Themes and Variations
The Drawings of Augustus John 1901-1931

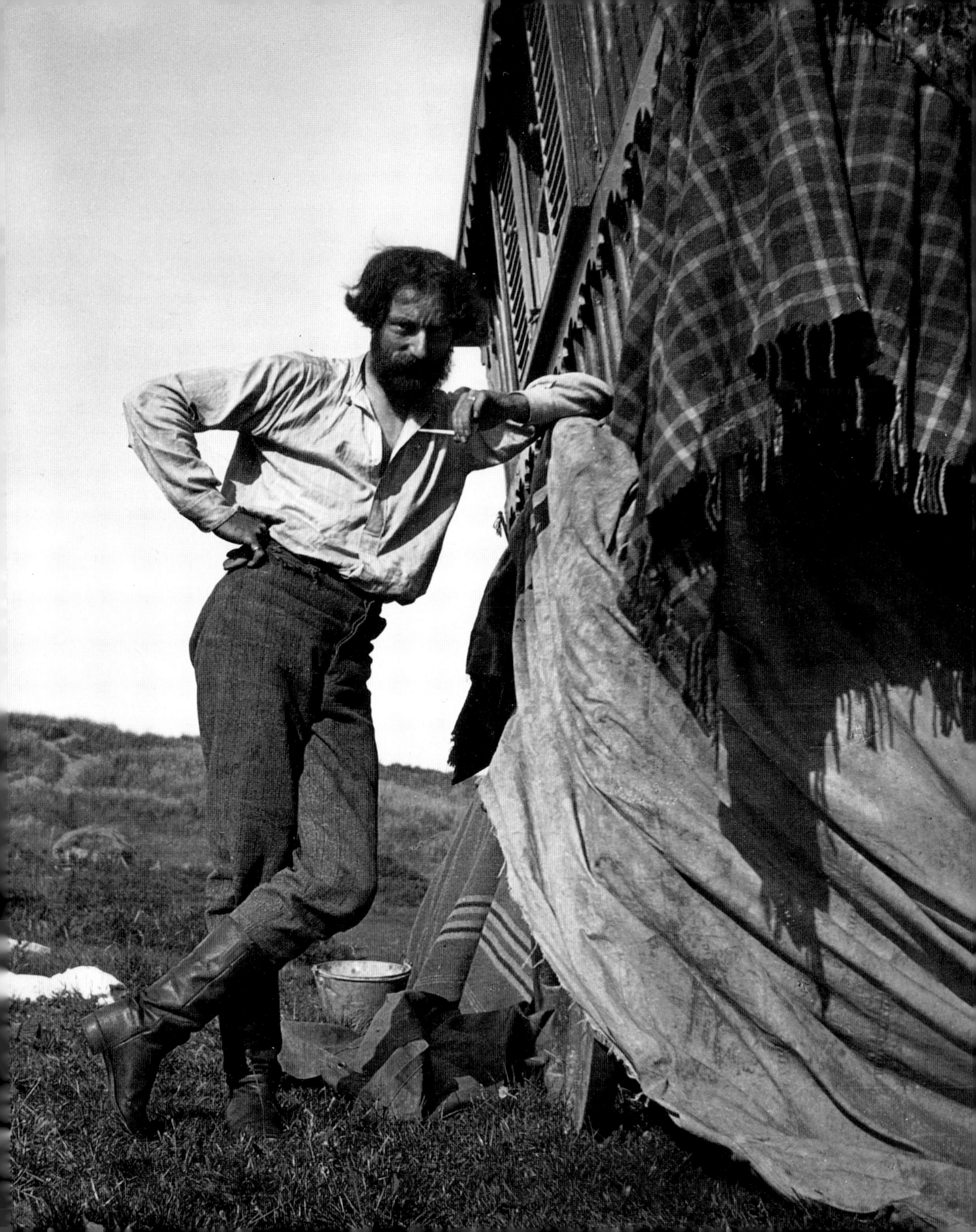

Themes and Variations

The Drawings of Augustus John 1901-1931

With Essays by Michael Holroyd,
Mark Evans and Rebecca John

Lund Humphries Publishers Ltd
in association with
National Museums & Galleries of Wales
and Spink & Son Ltd, London

First published in 1996 by
Lund Humphries Publishers Ltd
Park House
1 Russell Gardens
London NW11 9NN
in association with National Museums & Galleries of Wales
and Spink & Son Ltd
5 King Street, St James's, London SW1Y 6QS

Themes and Variations: The Drawings of Augustus John 1901-1931
© 1996 National Museums and Galleries of Wales
Texts © 1996 The Authors
Reproductions of works by Augustus John © 1996
Julius White

British Library Cataloguing in Publication Data
A catalogue record for this book is available from the British Library

Lund Humphries ISBN 0 85331 693 7
National Museums and Galleries of Wales ISBN 0 7200 0438 1

Typeset in Monotype Columbus
Made and printed in Great Britain by BAS Printers Limited
Over Wallop, Hampshire
Designed by Alan Bartram

Published to accompany the exhibition
Themes and Variations: The Drawings of Augustus John 1901-1931
National Museum & Gallery, Cardiff 20 July – 1 September 1996
Spink & Son Ltd, London 9 September – 4 October 1996
Royal Cambrian Academy, Conwy 2 November – 1 December 1996

Frontispiece
Augustus John leaning against the gypsy caravan, Norfolk, 1909

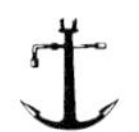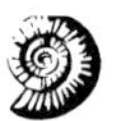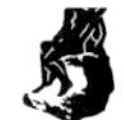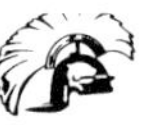

AMGUEDDFEYDD AC ORIELAU CENEDLAETHOL CYMRU
NATIONAL MUSEUMS & GALLERIES OF WALES

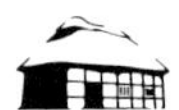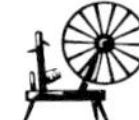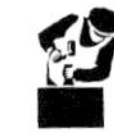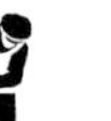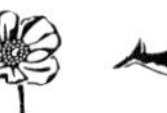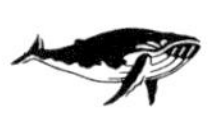

SPINK 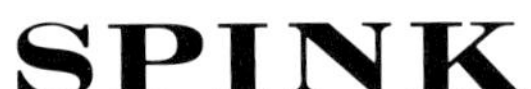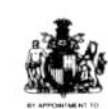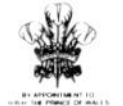

5 King Street, St James's, London SW1Y 6QS

Contents

6 Acknowledgements

6 Photographic Acknowledgements

7 Foreword

9 Augustus John and the art critics
by Michael Holroyd

13 Augustus John and art history
by Mark Evans

17 Colour plates

25 Augustus John and his subjects
by Rebecca John

28 Chronology

29 Catalogue

71 Select Bibliography

Acknowledgements

Photographic Acknowledgements

City of Aberdeen Art Gallery and
Museums Collection: Cat.65
Art Services Ltd: Cat.25
Ashmolean Museum, Oxford: Cat.39
City Museum and Art Gallery,
Birmingham: Cat.35
City of Bradford Metropolitan Council:
Cat.14
Bristol Museums and Art Gallery: Cat.40
The British Museum: Cat.34
Christie's: Cat.50
A. A. Edmunds: Cat.37
Fitzwilliam Museum, Cambridge: Cats 8,
13, 26-8, 30, 55, 58, 64
Glynn Vivian Art Gallery, Swansea:
Cat.56
Manchester City Art Galleries: Cats 10,
29, 47
National Museums and Galleries of
Wales: Cats 4, 11, 12, 15-18a, 20-3,
42-4, 60, 62, 68, figs 1-9
National Portrait Gallery: Cat.19
Spink & Son: Cats 3, 6, 7, 9, 24, 31-3, 36,
38, 46, 49, 52, 54, 57, 59, 67, 69-77
Tate Gallery: Cat.51
Whitworth Art Gallery, University of
Manchester: Cats 61, 63, 66
Witt Library, Courtauld Institute of Art:
Cats 1, 2, 5, 41, 45, 48, 53

This exhibition is another step in the continuing campaign to order and understand the vast legacy of Augustus John. Without the years of work dedicated to this task by David Fraser Jenkins, the late Malcolm Easton and Michael Holroyd, whose biography of the artist is indispensable, the job of co-ordinating the drawings would have been dauntingly complicated.

Many people have helped to make this exhibition possible. For assistance with loans, photographs and numerous requests for information, advice and support, special thanks are due to: Primrose Arnander; Caroline Bacon; Katy Barron; Hazel Berriman; Julia Blackburn; Ivor Braka; Alison Brown; Jackie Cartwright; Caroline Cuthbert; William Darby; D. Gareth Davies; Sir Brinsley Ford; Lady Gowrie; Richard Gray; Antony Griffiths; David Grover; Rosemary Harris; Alexander Hidalgo; Christine Hopper; Anna John; Susan Kent; Christopher Kingzett; Richard Kingzett; Vera Magyar; Rees Martin; Simon Mathews; Patrick Minns; Arthur Morgan; Robin Paisey; Janice Reading; Duncan Robinson; Max Rutherston; Anthony Sampson; Alison Samuel; James Slater; Elizabeth Smallwood; Alistair Smith; Thyrza Smith; Graham Southern; Sheena Stoddard; Maggie Stratton; Barbara Thompson; Christopher White; Stephen Wildman; Sarah Wimbush; Valerie Woulfe and Kai Kin Yung. At the National Museums and Galleries of Wales, thanks are due to: David Alston; Keith Bowen; Juliet Carey; Sue Cunningham; Cliff Darch; Lynette Edwards; Rosa Freeman; Arwel Hughes; Mike Jones; Kate Lowry; Christine Mackay; Bethany McIntyre; Colin Plain; Sylvia Richards and Kevin Thomas. This publication was realised by Alan Bartram, and John Taylor, Lucy Myers and Charlotte Burri of Lund Humphries. I have received every courtesy from the staff of Christie's, Sotheby's and the Courtauld Institute of Art.

For their enthusiastic commitment to this project I am deeply indebted to Karen Taylor and James Holland-Hibbert at Spink & Son, to Vicky Macdonald at the Royal Cambrian Academy and to my co-author Mark Evans at the National Museum and Gallery, Cardiff.

Rebecca John

Foreword

Gregarious, prolific and famed for his exceptional talent, Augustus John was lionised during the first half of this century, only to fall from favour during its second half. Arguably, his highest achievements were as a draughtsman. This exhibition assembles over seventy drawings and etchings to demonstrate how John's finest work came as a result of repeated studies of the same sitters – a procedure also used by his sister Gwen. It was John's granddaughter Rebecca John who first had the idea of basing an exhibition upon this working method, and our principal thanks go to her for her exemplary research and careful selection. She has also written the text of this publication, edited by Mark Evans.

It is especially appropriate that this exhibition should be a co-operative venture of the National Museums and Galleries of Wales, which first exhibited John's pictures in 1913 and has the largest collection of his work in existence, and Spink & Son, which has consistently dealt in his work for over fifty years. It is also highly fitting that the exhibition will be seen in North Wales at the Royal Cambrian Academy, of which John became President in 1934. The exhibition's opening coincides with the publication of the revised edition of John's biography by Michael Holroyd, who has contributed an essay to this publication.

This exhibition has been mounted with the generous support of Edwards Geldard Solicitors. It could not have been realised without the special understanding and generosity of our lenders, public and private; to them we extend our deepest gratitude.

Colin Ford CBE
Director
National Museums and Galleries of Wales

Anthony Spink
Chairman
Spink & Son

Augustus John and the art critics
Michael Holroyd

'You are reflecting whether it is not time to throw Augustus John, who has clearly become compromising, overboard', wrote Walter Sickert in *The Burlington Magazine* in 1916. 'Take my tip. Don't!'[1]

Yet Augustus John has been thrown overboard by many art critics today. In the first fifteen years of the twentieth century he was looked to, with admiration or opprobrium, as a leader of all that was progressive in British art. But recently he has vanished from the history of art in Britain to the extent of appearing only as the subject of a portrait by Matthew Smith in the exhibition of *British Art in the 20th Century: The Modern Movement* held by the Royal Academy in 1987. It is as if what Virginia Woolf had called in 1908 'the age of Augustus John'[2] never existed.

In the climate of the 1990s it is probably as well to remind readers of how critics and fellow artists regarded John's early work. 'We hardly dare confess how high are the hopes of Mr John's future which his paintings this year have led us to form', Roger Fry wrote in the *Athenaeum* towards the end of 1904. He would have to 'go back to Alfred Stevens or Etty or the youthful Watts',[3] Fry added, to find a fair comparison. Three years later John was sharing a notice with Rubens and Delacroix which Laurence Binyon contributed to the *Saturday Review*. In the United States, reviewing the famous Armory Show of 1913, James Huneker pointed to John, along with Matisse and Epstein, as the three big European talents.

Reacting to what *The Times* called John's 'uncanny notes of form and dashes of colour',[4] reactionary critics were equally extreme. 'At his worst he can outdo Gauguin',[5] one of them complained in 1910. For many he was the last word in incomprehensible modernity. 'After Picasso, Mr John.'[6]

But John's fellow artists, among them Surrealists, Futurists and Vorticists, looked on him as their fugleman. He had a magnetic power over his contemporaries. 'I think John's talent and daring is an excellent example for us', the portrait painter Neville Lytton wrote to William Rothenstein in 1908, 'and shows us in what direction it is expedient for us to throw our bonnets over the windmills'.[7] Paul Nash, who singled out his 'technical power', confessed to 'a deep respect for John's draughtsmanship especially when it was applied with a paint brush';[8] C. R. W. Nevinson, who called him 'a genius', wrote that 'though I am always called a Modern, I have always tried to base myself on John's example';[9] and Wyndham Lewis, despite mocking him for having become 'an institution like Madame Tussaud's', praised John for having, as the legitimate successor of Aubrey Beardsley, buried 'the mock naturalists and pseudo-impressionists'.[10]

John's work began to change in the First World War and went rapidly downhill in the 1930s. He found no new subject-matter and he abused his technique. 'I have always been an enthusiastic admirer of John's work', Roger Fry had written in the *Nation* in December 1910.[11] But seven years later Fry was telling Vanessa Bell that he found John 'almost entirely stupid'[12] about modern pictures after a visit to the Omega Workshops. For the most part, however, John's later inferior work did not blind critics to his earlier merits. Looking back over forty years of his draughtsmanship at the National Gallery in 1940, Herbert Read paid tribute to his 'superb mastery of form', his 'balance of psychological insight and formal harmony', and concluded that it was 'doubtful if any other contemporary artist in Europe could display such virtuosity and skill'.[13]

One of the first writers to attempt a survey of John's career, reconciling the apparent contradictions, was Anthony Blunt. 'Everyone is agreed on the fact that Augustus John was born with a quite exceptional talent for painting – some even use the word genius – and almost everyone is agreed that he has in some way wasted it', Blunt wrote in the *Spectator* in 1938. John's greatest works, akin to that of masters from the past, were his portrait heads, usually done in two coloured chalks at the beginning of the century, Blunt argued. 'These early drawings have a sort of industrious observation which distinguishes them from all the later productions. For even in the oil sketches of the next period John is already letting himself go in a sort of mannerism, though the mannerism is so brilliant that one is at first willing to accept it as a serious basis for painting.' What Blunt finally objected to was the accelerated, almost baroque, method of painting John adopted which helped him to outpace the growing doubts and hesitations from which he sometimes attempted to divert attention by over-emphatic gesture and rhetoric – most famously in the full-length profile portrait of Madame Suggia of 1920-3 (Tate Gallery). John's technical brilliance 'will stand the most minute study, and even study over a long period, without becoming thin', he wrote. 'It is only in his methods of dealing with the psychological problems presented by his sitters that his shorthand appears.'

The portraits and figure studies from the 1920s onwards lost the brilliance of the earlier paintings without regaining the meticulous care of the early drawings. 'It is only because his gifts are so great that one is forced to judge him by the very highest that he seems to fail', Blunt concluded.[14]

In contrast to Fry, Read and Blunt; to Paul Nash, C. R. W. Nevinson, Wyndham Lewis and others in the first half of the century came the wholesale dismissal led by Geoffrey Grigson in the mid-1970s. John was transformed into a *pasticheur*. His oils were seen as 'flashy and inferior' and his draughtsmanship no more than 'simulacra of the genuine'. Under such treatment, John dwindled into a 'vulgar art-school draughtsman with a provincial mind'[15] whose drawings were uncreative and impersonal and whose paintings lacked imagination.

At the end of the twentieth century we are left in a quandary. Was John's high reputation a product of the insularity and delusion of the English art world which lasted into the 1930s? Or has the posthumous decline of that reputation been, in the words of Grey Gowrie, 'a quirk of our own time'?[16]

There are several factors that have dramatised this decline. The very necessary re-evaluation of his sister Gwen John's work, which began seriously in 1968 with a touring exhibition organised by the Arts Council, has been conducted somewhat unnecessarily at the expense of Augustus John – not by Gwen John scholars such as Cecily Langdale or Mary Taubman, but by journalists obliged to submit to the aggressive simplicities of a competitive age. In addition, the mass of indifferent work dumped on to the market through the posthumous studio sales of 1962-3, which has continued haphazardly to surface ever since, further depressed estimates of his worth.

In his monograph on Augustus John published in 1979, Richard Shone likened his career to those of Thomas Lawrence, David Wilkie and John Everett Millais, all 'artists who began very well and ended very badly'. John's talent was predominantly lyrical, Shone argued, and he interpreted the English, Welsh and French landscape through poetic or visionary eyes. 'This lyrical mode belongs essentially to youth (as so often in poetry) and it is rare', Shone wrote, '... for the artist to effect a successful transformation as he grows older.'[17]

Such a transformation was made more difficult by the misapprehension of his talent and temperament by his contemporaries. As early as 1900, Charles Conder decided that 'large decoration ... seems to be his forte'.[18] Nine years later, Roger Fry was writing in *The Burlington Magazine*: 'In Watts we sacrificed to our incurable individualism, our national incapacity of co-operating for ideal ends, a great monumental designer. A generous fate has given us another chance in Mr John ...'[19] There are one or two good examples of John's large-scale composition, notably the impressive if incomplete *Lyric fantasy* (Tate Gallery) and the more eloquent *Childhood of Pyramus* once owned by Clive and Vanessa Bell (Johannesburg Art Gallery). But for the most part these big decorations were disappointing and sometimes disastrous. The mural he was commissioned to paint for the Irish art patron Sir Hugh Lane, called 'Forza e amore', he went on to destroy; and the vast triptych over which he laboured many of his last years came to nothing. Those that were completed, such as *The mumpers* (Detroit Art Gallery), often appear as artificial essays in the manner of Puvis de Chavannes, unhappily blended with some aspects of modernity, revealing John's inability to organise large groups of people. Yet he went on longing to paint on the heroic scale. 'When one thinks of painting on great expanses of wall, painting of any other kind seems hardly worth doing',[20] he said to John Rothenstein in 1939. No wonder Joyce Carey used John as one of his models for the bohemian artist Gulley Jimson in his novel *The Horse's Mouth* (1944).

In fact John was happier drawing and painting single figures on a comparatively small scale – his oil panels are seldom larger than 15 × 12 inches. In this he resembled his sister Gwen, acknowledging late in life the strange fact that 'Gwen and I were not opposites but much the same really, but we took a different attitude'.[21] What they shared was an unbridgeable loneliness interrupted by desperate infatuations – at least once for the same person. Gwen tried to come to terms with her solitude by living alone, almost in exile, in Paris. Augustus tried to lose his sense of loneliness with a large complicated family and amid a crowded London life. They also shared a sense of impatience, both believing that a picture should be finished in one or two sittings. But Gwen prepared for this fast working practice with meticulous care, while Augustus attempted to achieve it through an intense 'fit of seeing'. His paintings, when they became larger, became emptier; hers grew smaller and eventually vanished altogether. It was as if they had the same telescope but were looking through different ends of it.

Gwen was aged eight and Augustus six when their mother died. She had been an amateur painter, and the determination with which son and daughter took up her gift says something about its origins and their obsessive choice of subjects. In Gwen's empty chair beside an open window, in her vacant rooms, we can feel her isolation; her women alone, her children sometimes facing away from us in church, have a poignancy enhanced by their obliqueness; her flowers and cats are containable love objects. All are indoor subjects. Augustus used outdoor subjects: women poised against the sky with their children or planted like trees in the landscape, raggle-taggle families of wanderers, all reflecting an ideal life as in some ballet, the focus of his wish fulfilment.

Neither of them were anecdotal artists, but Gwen's subjects leave you with the impression of a story told, a story with a sad ending in which all of us are implicated. Augustus' pictures are aesthetic statements, sudden sightings of the *dramatis personae* before the drama begins. Contrasting them in her survey of the fortunes of women painters and their work, *The Obstacle Race*, Germaine Greer explains that Gwen John moved away from the virtuoso beginnings she shared with her brother 'forever compressing and concentrating her art and her feelings to one inner end', while Augustus John's 'marvellous facility' stranded him in 'superficiality'.[22] In literature, superficiality is almost inevitably a pejorative term, but in painting not so. It was the profundity of the superficial Augustus John explored. For as Oscar Wilde reminds us: 'It is only shallow people who do not judge from appearances. The mystery of the world is the visible, not the invisible.'[23]

In his *Modern English Painters*, John Rothenstein recalled seeing Augustus peering fixedly, 'almost obsessively, at pictures by Gwen as though he could discern in them his own temperament in reverse; as though he could derive from the act satisfaction in his own wider range, greater natural endowment, tempestuous energy, and at the same time be reproached by her single-mindedness, her steadiness of focus, above all by the sureness with which she attained her simpler aims.'[24]

The testimony of Augustus' admiration for Gwen's pictures extends over fifty years. 'I am flummoxed by their beauty',[25] he wrote to his son Edwin a year after her death in 1939. But what did she think of his pictures? 'I think them rather good', she wrote to their Slade School friend Ursula Tyrwhitt at the beginning of the First World War. 'They want something that will come soon!'[26]

The selection and arrangement of this exhibition is an attempt to suggest what Augustus John's pictures 'wanted', and to bring art critics of the past and present on to common ground. His full-length drawings of Ida, one hand on hip, another held parallel to the ground and disappearing off the paper, out of the frame; and of Dorelia, with one arm draped over her head and the other leaning against the frame, are preparing to take their places in the rhythmical arc of figures for the large decoration called *The way down to the sea*. Similarly, the Equihen fishergirl sitting with her elbows angled out or standing with her back to us is destined for another decoration planned on the north coast of France. All of them resemble dancers in rehearsal, preparing for the curtain to go up.

Augustus John's portrait heads speak for themselves. But this series of variations tells us something new. They replace the legendary facility of someone who, with a swish of the pencil, went from one flash in the pan to another, and present in its place evidence of an obsessive observation and industry, like the drawings 'often repeated dozens of times, with slight variations'[27] of his sister Gwen.

Notes

Abbreviated bibliographic references are to works listed in the Select Bibliography on pp.71-2.

1 'O Matre Pulchra!', *The Burlington Magazine*, vol.29, April 1916, p.34; collected in *A Free House!* (ed. Osbert Sitwell), London 1947, p.197

2 Quentin Bell, *Virginia Woolf. A Biography*, vol.1, London 1972, p.124

3 *Athenaeum*, 19 November 1904, p.700

4 *The Times*, 5 December 1910

5 *The Queen*, 10 December 1910

6 *Illustrated London News*, 30 December 1912

7 William Rothenstein, *Men and Memories*, vol.2, London 1932, p.136

8 Paul Nash, *Outline*, London 1949, p.7

9 C. R. W. Nevinson, *Paint and Prejudice*, London 1937, p.189

10 Wyndham Lewis, 'History of the Largest Independent Society in England', *Blast No.2* (July 1915); see *Wyndham Lewis on Art. Collected Writings 1913-1956* (ed. Walter Michel and C. J. Fox), London 1969, p.91

11 'A Postscript on Post-Impressionism', *Nation*, 24 December 1910

12 *Letters of Roger Fry*, vol.2 (ed. Denys Sutton), London 1972, p.404

13 *The Burlington Magazine*, vol.78, January 1941, p.3

14 'Art. Augustus John', *Spectator*, 27 May 1938

15 'Romany Flash', *Blessings, Kicks and Curses*, London 1982, pp.203-7

16 'The Twentieth Century', *The Genius of British Painting* (ed. David Piper 1975), London, p.302

17 Shone 1979, p.3

18 Holroyd 1996, p.82

19 *The Burlington Magazine*, vol.15, April 1909, p.17

20 John Rothenstein, *Modern English Painters*, vol.1, *Sickert to Smith*, London 1976, p.184

21 John Rothenstein, *Time's Thievish Progress. Autobiography*, III, London 1970, p.21

22 Germaine Greer, *The Obstacle Race. The Fortunes of Women Painters and their Work*, New York 1979, p.110

23 *The Picture of Dorian Gray*, Chapter 2

24 *Modern English Painters*, vol. 1, *Sickert to Smith*, London 1976, pp.160-1

25 Augustus John to Edwin John, 7 May 1940, National Library of Wales, 22312C ff. 28-9

26 Gwen John to Ursula Tyrwhitt, 31 December 1917. Partially quoted in Susan Chitty, *Gwen John*, London 1981, p.148; National Library of Wales, 14930C

27 *Finishing Touches* 1964, p.81

Augustus John and art history
Mark Evans

Augustus John never attempted a strictly art-historical essay, but his articles for *Vogue*, his short notes for *The Burlington Magazine*, his autobiographical fragments *Chiaroscuro* and *Finishing Touches* and his correspondence shed considerable light on his attitude towards artists of his own day and past masters.[1] His introduction to a major retrospective of his drawings at the National Gallery in 1940 began with a celebrated quotation from Ingres, 'Le dessin, c'est la probité de l'art' ('Drawing is the probity of art'), and the exhibition included a 'study from Rembrandt' and the 'study after Watteau' with which he had won a prize while a student.[2] John admitted that at the Slade 'I was early imbued with a proper reverence for the Masters … by frequentation of the British Museum and other collections', and with a particular regard for Rubens, Michelangelo, Rembrandt, Watteau and Ingres.[3] His enthusiasm for the 'terrible, mysterious Spaniard' El Greco was tempered by the latter's 'mawkish religiosity' and he found Goya's *Majas* vulgar in comparison with Rubens' *Three Graces* and Titian's *Venus*, which 'seemed to me a dream of noble luxury'.[4]

Ridiculing young artists unable 'to accept the validity of the European tradition of painting, and recognise … the pre-eminence of Rembrandt as a draughtsman', John argued that the abiding significance of Paris lay in its past masters, from the Impressionists and Post-Impressionists to earlier painters from Courbet and Ingres to Largillière and Fouquet.[5] He expressed rather perfunctory admiration for the Northern and Italian primitives, but in 1941 argued that Holbein, Van Eyck and Botticelli embodied 'the outline we are all in search of, and which may yet delineate the "shapes of things to come"'.[6] While the art of the past provided a store of vital precepts, it presented dangers: 'The aspiring student who thinks he may best find himself by pursuing the Old Masters, is in grave danger of losing sight of his guides as well as his goal … Fidelity to venerable traditions too consistently practised and for too long may rob him of his fire and end in impotence … The conjuration of an illustrious name, instead of fortifying, may only corrupt the student's innocence and damp his courage so that he sinks into the false security of precedent and the second hand.'[7]

In 1911-12 John wrote to the American collector John Quinn, expressing appreciation of Van Gogh, Gauguin, Cézanne, Renoir, Degas, Toulouse-Lautrec and Anquetin.[8] He had a high regard for Daumier and liked Van Gogh's early, dark Belgian paintings as much as his better-known late works.[9] Although he damned Maurice Denis with faint praise and regarded Matisse 'with the utmost suspicion', he endorsed Picasso as a 'genius, albeit of a morbid sort' for his 'Blue Period' works in which he recognised the influence of Daumier.[10] John retained fond memories of Modigliani.[11] He bought two stone heads from the artist and was moved to paint a still-life titled *In memoriam Amedeo Modigliani* (private collection) after his death, which he referred to eight years later as 'still a recent tragedy'.[12]

During a visit to Germany in 1925 John met Liebermann and took an interest in the works of Hans von Marées, but the only major German painter he knew well was Oskar Kokoschka, who occupied a neighbouring studio in Paris in 1930.[13] In 1928 he saluted the Impressionists and 'the later romantics

… known to the English reader as Post-Impressionists', while dismissing contemporary Paris as 'the world's greatest stock exchange for art'.[14] John found Marie Laurencin 'delightful … but tiresome', Derain 'sometimes less than pedantic; and more rarely more' and 'the Andalusian prodigy' Picasso 'more meretricious day by day'.[15] He was impressed by Segonzac and Othon Friesz and considered the older artists Forain, Rouault and Bonnard 'individual and isolated examples of the glory of French painting'.[16] Discarding his earlier suspicion, he described Matisse as 'the best, the most sensitive, of French painters'.[17]

While retaining his regard for his old teacher Wilson Steer, John acknowledged that his work had gradually 'lost the adventurous and surprising character which had excited and charmed me so at first'.[18] He respectfully recalled the excitement aroused by a visit from Whistler, the latter's appreciation of old-master painting and his praise of Gwen John's 'fine sense of *tone*'.[19] His cool attitude towards 'young Walter Sickert' reveals offence with the latter's disloyalty towards his old master Whistler.[20] In 1928 John called for a reappraisal of the Whistlerian painters Paul Maitland and W. E. Osborne.[21] Reflecting on Whistler's banishment of the last vestiges of 'pre-Raphaelite romanticism', he acknowledged that, in its turn, 'His meticulous aestheticism has given place to a wider and more robust treatment … due probably to the fresh fields of inspiration derived from older and more exotic civilisations'.[22] Having been initially repelled by the primitivism of Epstein and Gill, John later cited with approval five examples 'of the modern painter, who finds healthy nourishment from a diet furnished impartially by Aztecs, Persians, cave-men and even negroes'; Matthew Smith, Henry Lamb, Duncan Grant, Vanessa Bell and the Russian mosaicist Boris Anrep.[23]

The remark 'Belonging to no particular camp, I had a footing in all' characterised John's attitude towards the Camden Town Group in specific and his contemporaries in general.[24] The major exception was his relationship with his fellow Welshman and Slade graduate J. D. Innes in 1910-13. John recommended Innes to Quinn as an 'entirely original chap and that's saying a lot' and recalled how he had been introduced by him to the landscape of North Wales.[25] One of John's longest essays on a single artist was on another young Welsh painter, Evan Walters.[26] Contrasting the 'unimpassioned realism' of Walters' paintings of life in the Welsh mining towns with the work of Daumier and the young Van Gogh, he observed: 'This independence, which … even benefited from the menacing neighbourhood of the Royal Academy, withstood risks equally severe when he returned to his native surroundings. It is difficult for anyone who has not lived in a Welsh provincial district to realise the almost heart-breaking conditions of an artist's life there.'[27] Written shortly before his election as a Royal Academician, these lines have a distinctly autobiographical quality.

John had some sympathy for modernism. Of Picasso, he admitted: 'If his earlier cubistic experiments now appear to me unamusing, I cannot forget the power, wit and ingenuity which subjugated me once as I faced a two-dimensional adumbration of the *Commedia dell'Arte*.'[28] His valediction to the recently deceased Wyndham Lewis criticises the polemical stance rather than the content of Vorticism and refers affectionately to 'the only incurable cubist in London … the gifted William Roberts'.[29] In an essay on the philosopher Charles Fourier, John imagined an Utopian city dominated by a monumental stone figure of a woman by Henry Moore.[30] However, after visiting

Amsterdam in 1930, he contrasted 'the huge blocks of modern apartments' with 'the tall narrow houses which … used to line the old canals' and concluded that 'the new Germanic developments belong to a world in which I should always feel a stranger'.[31] In similar language John acknowledged that, despite listening to 'the airy bellowings of my friend Victor Pasmore', abstraction remained 'a cult to which I had to admit myself a stranger'.[32]

The opinions expressed by John on earlier art are broadly consistent with the sources of techniques and motifs in his own work. As a student he was attracted, like Wilson Steer, by sixteenth-century mannerism, as is apparent from the ambitious composition *Moses and the Brazen Serpent* (Slade School of Fine Art, London) with which he won the summer painting competition at the Slade in 1898.[33] His early drawings display a method of hatching learned from Watteau and the more linear handling of Ingres, while his taste for red and black chalk drawings was conditioned by the study of Michelangelo and Rubens.[34] The example of Rembrandt was central to John's etchings.[35] His paintings of 1901-4 include citations from Rubens, Velasquez, Ingres, Hals and, perhaps, Manet.[36] When called upon to paint *Chaloner Dowdall as Lord Mayor of Liverpool* (National Gallery of Victoria, Melbourne) in 1909, John approached the unfamiliar genre of a monumental civic portrait via Van Dyck's State portraits of Charles I, which typically include an elongated figure of the monarch accompanied by a subordinate.[37] The brilliant small oils painted following his visit to Italy and Provence in 1910 incorporate references to Quattrocento painting.[38] Following his first visit to Spain in 1922 the influence of El Greco was profound, retaining its impact as late as 1942-3.[39]

John's relationship with his immediate predecessors and contemporaries is more elusive. The poetic figure compositions of nude and clothed females and the groups of gypsies in landscape settings which he produced during the decade before the First World War took their starting point, respectively, from the mural decorations of Puvis de Chavannes and the *saltimbanques* of Daumier.[40] His flirtation with primitivism in 1907-15 was indebted to Gauguin and Picasso.[41] The addition of flat washes of colour to pencil drawings used by John from 1906 was probably learned from the watercolours of Rodin, while his portrait of *Gustav Stresemann* (Albright Knox Art Gallery, Buffalo), painted at Berlin in 1925, hints tantalisingly at the influence of German 'New Realist' artists.[42] His only close working relationship was with J. D. Innes. They painted together for several years, producing small landscapes with fresh colours separated by a narrow reserve, over a pencil outline on panel. While it is impossible to isolate what each learned from the other, John's appreciation of Innes' prodigious activity and rapid method suggests that, in the matter of technique, the younger artist was the senior partner.[43]

Commentators rapidly recognised John's debt to the old masters. In 1916 Hugh Blaker argued that '[in the present] era of the distinguished artist who cannot draw', John's unique skill as a draughtsman stemmed directly from his 'appreciation of the work of the past'; a quality which he shared with Daumier, the Barbizon School and the Impressionists.[44] In 1920 Campbell Dodgson took him to task for 'lack of concentration and acquiescence in an apparent finish', while defending his recourse to work of the past: 'John has learnt much from the old masters, but that fact does not make him either their equal or their plagiarist'.[45] He concluded: 'his art will live … by the vivid

Notes

Abbreviated bibliographic references are to works listed in the Select Bibliography on pp.71-2.

1 'The Paintings of Evan Walters', 'The Unknown Artist', 'The Woman Artist', 'Paris and the Painter', 'Three English Artists', 'Some Contemporary French Painters', 'Five Modern Artists', 'Interior Decoration', *Vogue* 1928; 'A Note on Holbein', *The Burlington Magazine* 1941; 'A Note on Rembrandt', *The Burlington Magazine* 1942; *Chiaroscuro* 1952; *Finishing Touches* 1964; *Autobiography* 1975

2 exh. London 1940, pp.17-19

3 *ibid*; *Autobiography* p.50

4 Holroyd 1996, pp.342 and 484; *Autobiography*, pp.164, 204 and 424-6

5 *ibid*, p.419; 'Paris and the Painter', pp.46-72

6 *Autobiography*, pp.55, 120, 150-1 and 333; 'A Note on Holbein', p.266

7 *Autobiography*, p.418

8 Holroyd 1996, pp.341-4

9 *ibid*, pp.78-9 and 341; *Autobiography*, pp.240-1

10 Holroyd 1996, p.342; *Autobiography*, pp.80-1

11 *ibid*, pp.148-9

12 'Some Contemporary French Painters', p.47; Easton and Holroyd 1974, pp.172-3

13 *Autobiography*, pp.161-4 and 244; *Oskar Kokoschka 1886-1980*, Tate Gallery, London 1986, p.350

14 'Some Contemporary French Painters', p.37; 'Paris and the Painter', p.46; Holroyd 1996, p.345

15 'The Woman Artist', p.80; 'Some Contemporary French Painters', p.37

16 *ibid*, p.60; Holroyd 1996, pp.344-5

17 'Some Contemporary French Painters', p.37; Holroyd 1996, p.344

18 *Autobiography*, pp.51-2

19 *ibid*, p.57 and 78

20 *ibid*, p.58; Holroyd 1996, pp.94 and 173n

21 'Three English Artists', pp.44-5 and 75

22 'Five Modern Artists', p.76

23 *ibid*, pp.76, 77 and 104

24 *Autobiography*, p.90

25 *ibid*, pp.227-30; Holroyd 1996, pp.345-7

26 'The Paintings of Evan Walters', p.40

27 *ibid*, p.41

28 *Autobiography*, p.81

29 *ibid*, pp.406-12

30 *ibid*, p.218

31 *ibid*, p.240

32 *ibid*, p.419

33 exh. Cardiff 1978, nos 1-3

34 exh. Cardiff 1988, pp.14-15; exh. Cardiff 1978, no.22; and compare *Drawings by Michelangelo*, British Museum, London 1975, nos 112, 114 and 119 and *Rubens Drawings and Sketches*, British Museum, London 1977, nos 154 and 155

35 Campbell Dodgson 1920, pp.x-xi

36 exh. Cardiff 1988, pp.16 and 28; Easton and Holroyd 1974, pp.50-5

37 Easton and Holroyd 1974, pp.142-3; and compare *The Late King's Goods* (ed. A. MacGregor), London and Oxford 1989, pp.198-9

38 Easton and Holroyd 1974, pp.17 and 68-9. Likely prototypes for John's *Pyramus* include

insight, and skill of hand as well as eye, with which he records some being that he has actually seen, be it a pony grazing on Dartmoor, or a *Romani Chai* ..., a model posed for the nude, a girl whose eyes have bewitched him for a moment, or a woman whom he has loved'.[46] Roger Fry, himself a specialist in Italian Renaissance art, was an early enthusiast for John's work. He applauded a 'new reverence to the art of the past' among progressive British painters in 1905; although it has been pointed out that the critic was actually seeking a new academicism applicable to modern times.[47] John noted drily that both 'Henry Tonks of the Slade and Roger Fry, the Cézannist' were 'doctrinaires' who 'believed in cultivating the Old Masters – a thing which at that time [1914] was simply not done!'[48]

Despite his enduring fame, only a handful of serious studies of John's art have appeared. Various factors have contributed to this. His best works, executed prior to 1920, are considerably outweighed by the generally indifferent productions of his last forty years. In the environment of the *avant-garde*, the late work of its longer-lived exponents, especially those who later came to terms with academic art, has an inherent tendency to be discounted; as is indicated by the examples of Corot and J. E. Millais, or De Chirico and Henry Moore. There is the objection that John's subject-matter was essentially superficial, lacking in 'fundamental brainwork', in Dodgson's words, and the moral complaint that 'he was born with a quite exceptional talent ... and ... has in some way wasted it', as Anthony Blunt put it.[49] John's equivocal attitude to the First Post-Impressionist Exhibition and his refusal to exhibit in the Second have been interpreted as a fundamental rejection of the modern movement which branded him permanently as a reactionary.[50] Most telling of all is his incompatibility with the modernist model of art history, which charts the progress of organised, theoretically based movements, and only accommodates rogue individuals – such as Stanley Spencer or Matthew Smith – who can be linked with earlier visionaries or an unimpeachable continental source. And yet, as the century nears its end, the history of twentieth-century British art looks less like the triumphal progress of international modernism than the periodic reassertion of an insular, painterly figuration, distrustful of theoretical systems and deeply attached to the past. The drawings in this exhibition represent a major contribution to this tradition.

portraits in the National Gallery by Antonello da Messina and Botticelli; see J. Dunkerton *et al*, *Giotto to Dürer*, New Haven, London and Oxford 1991, pp.198-9

39 Bertram 1923, p.16 and pl.19; exh. Cardiff 1988, pp.53 and 55

40 exh. Cardiff 1978, pp.4-5; Easton and Holroyd 1974, p.13

41 exh. Cardiff 1978, nos 116-17; Easton and Holroyd 1974, pp.21 and 58-9

42 exh. Cardiff 1978, p.4; exh. Cardiff 1988, p.35

43 Holroyd 1996, p.355; *Autobiography*, p.228

44 'The Drawings of Augustus John', p.122ff. A dealer and former curator of the Holburne of Menstrie Museum, Bath, Blaker was an art advisor to the Davies sisters of Gregynog, whose distinguished collection of paintings by Daumier, Millet and Impressionist and Post-Impressionist artists was largely assembled in 1908-20. In 1916-18 the sisters

also made a major series of purchases of works by Augustus John; exh. Cardiff 1988, p.9

45 Campbell Dodgson 1920, p.x. From 1893 Assistant Keeper and from 1912 Keeper of the Department of Prints and Drawings at the British Museum, Dodgson probably became acquainted with John during the latter's student visits

46 *Ibid*, p.xi

47 A. Causey, 'Formalism and the Figurative Tradition in British Painting', *British Art in the 20th Century: The Modern Movement* (ed. S. Compton), Munich and London 1986, p.16

48 *Autobiography*, p.408

49 *ibid*; A. Blunt, 'Augustus John', *The Spectator*, 27 May 1938, p.961

50 Holroyd 1996, pp.341-7, where it is pointed out that John was considerably more sympathetic towards these exhibitions than is usually realised

Ida, study for 'The way down to the sea',
*c.*1902-6, pencil on blue paper (Cat.7)

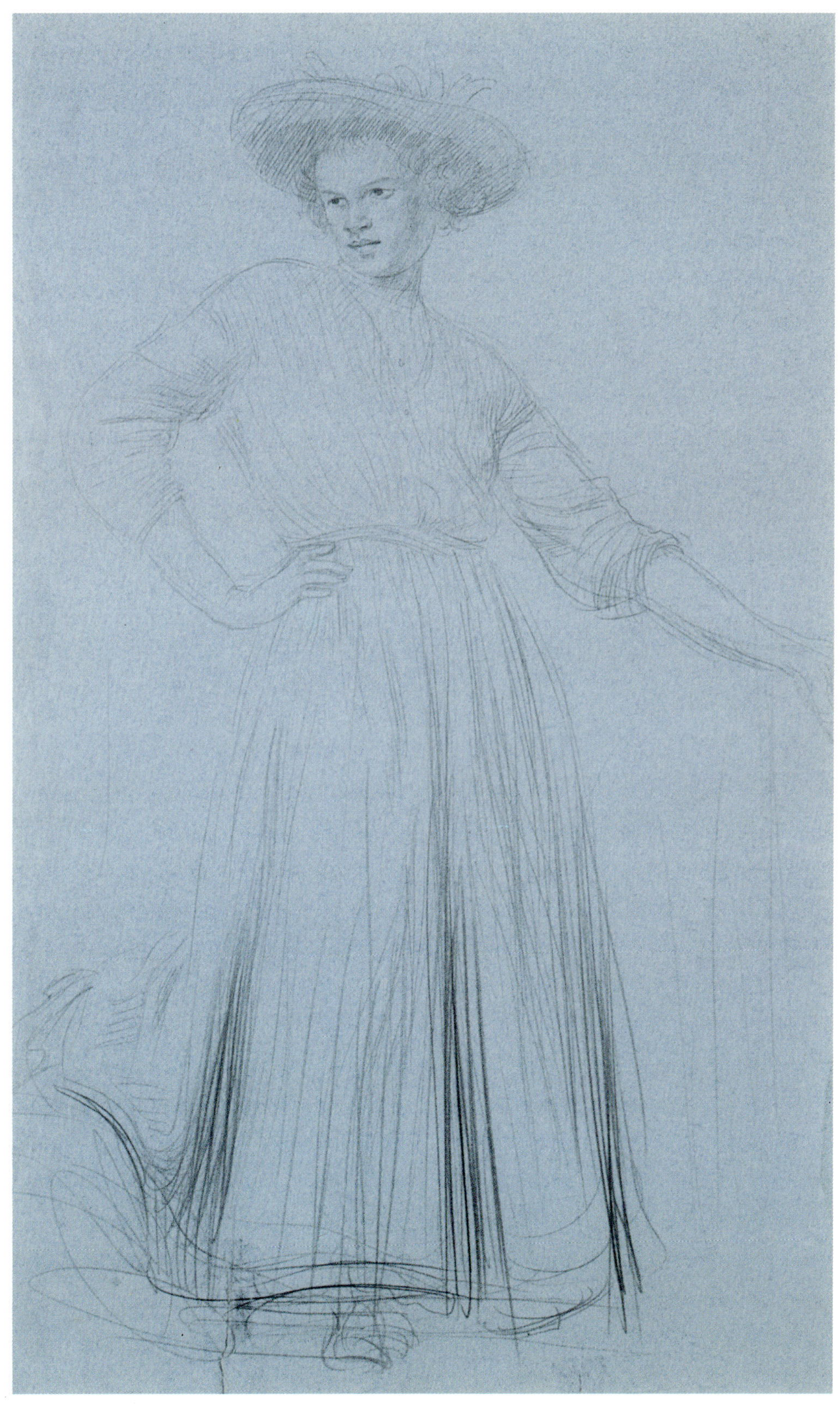

Plate 2
Study of Dorelia, head and shoulders,
1903, red and black chalk on pale grey paper (Cat.9)

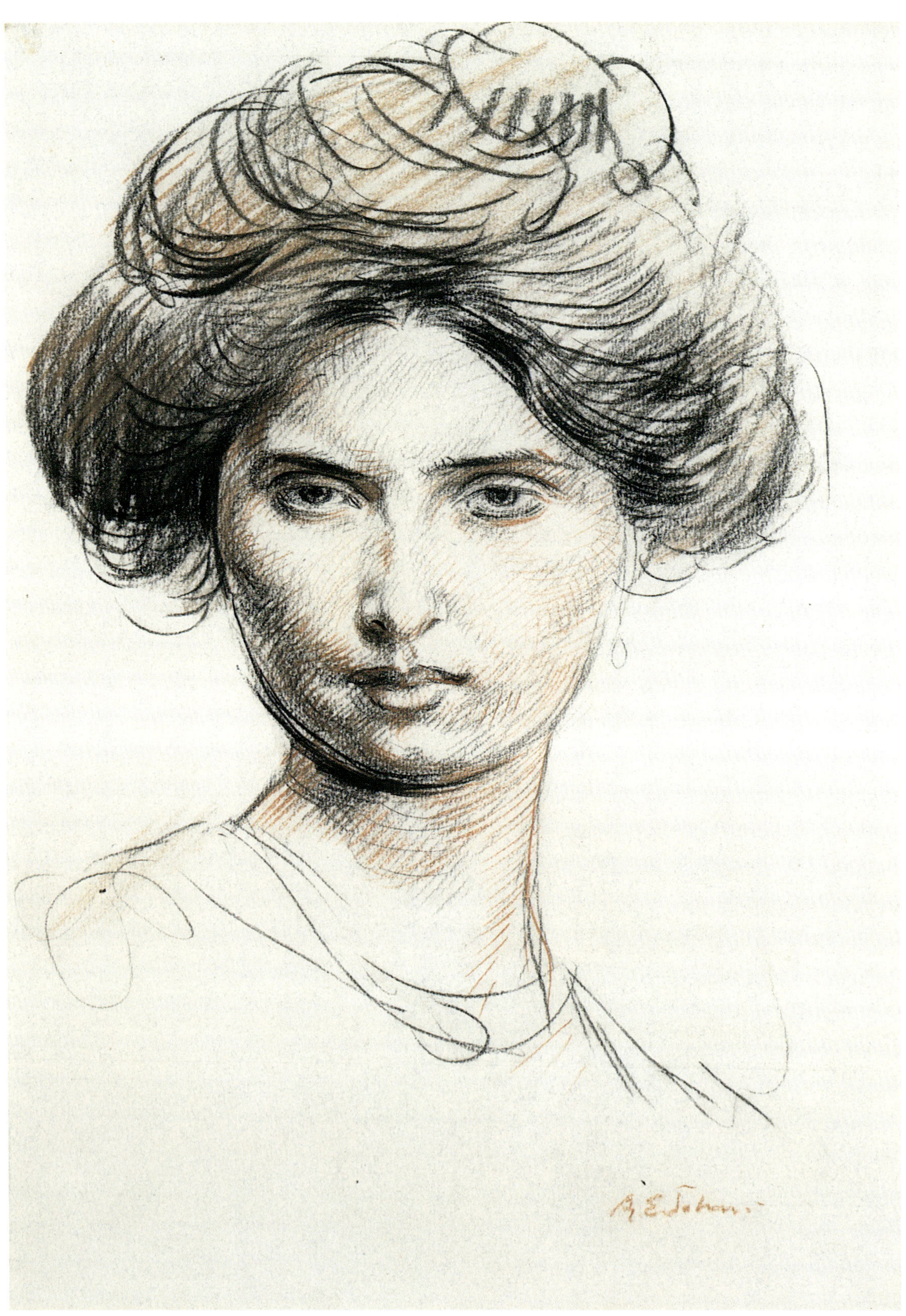

Plate 3
Dorelia wearing a hat,
*c.*1904-6, dark red chalk (Cat.13)

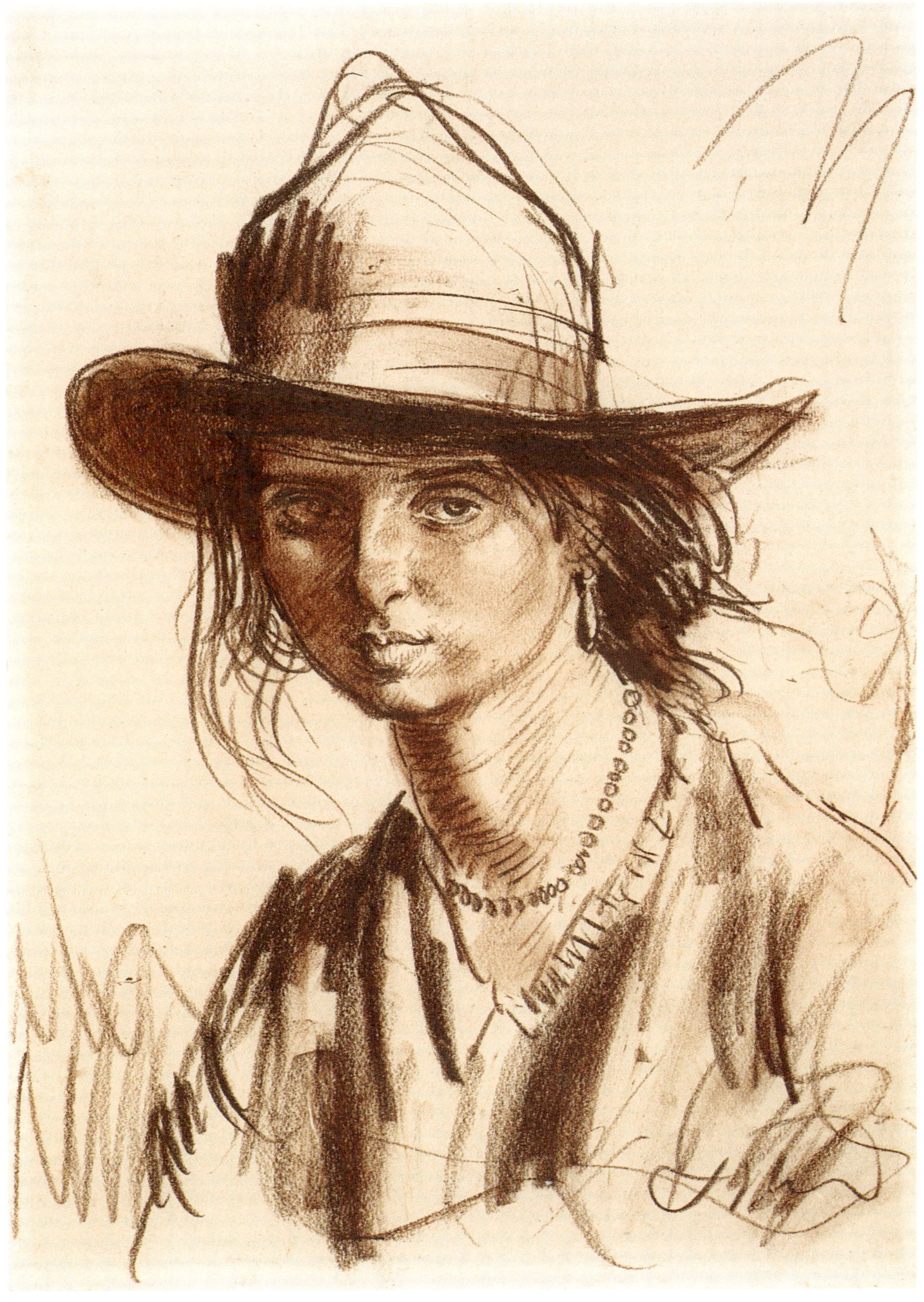

Plate 4
Dorelia with earrings, 1907,
1907, red chalk (Cat.32)

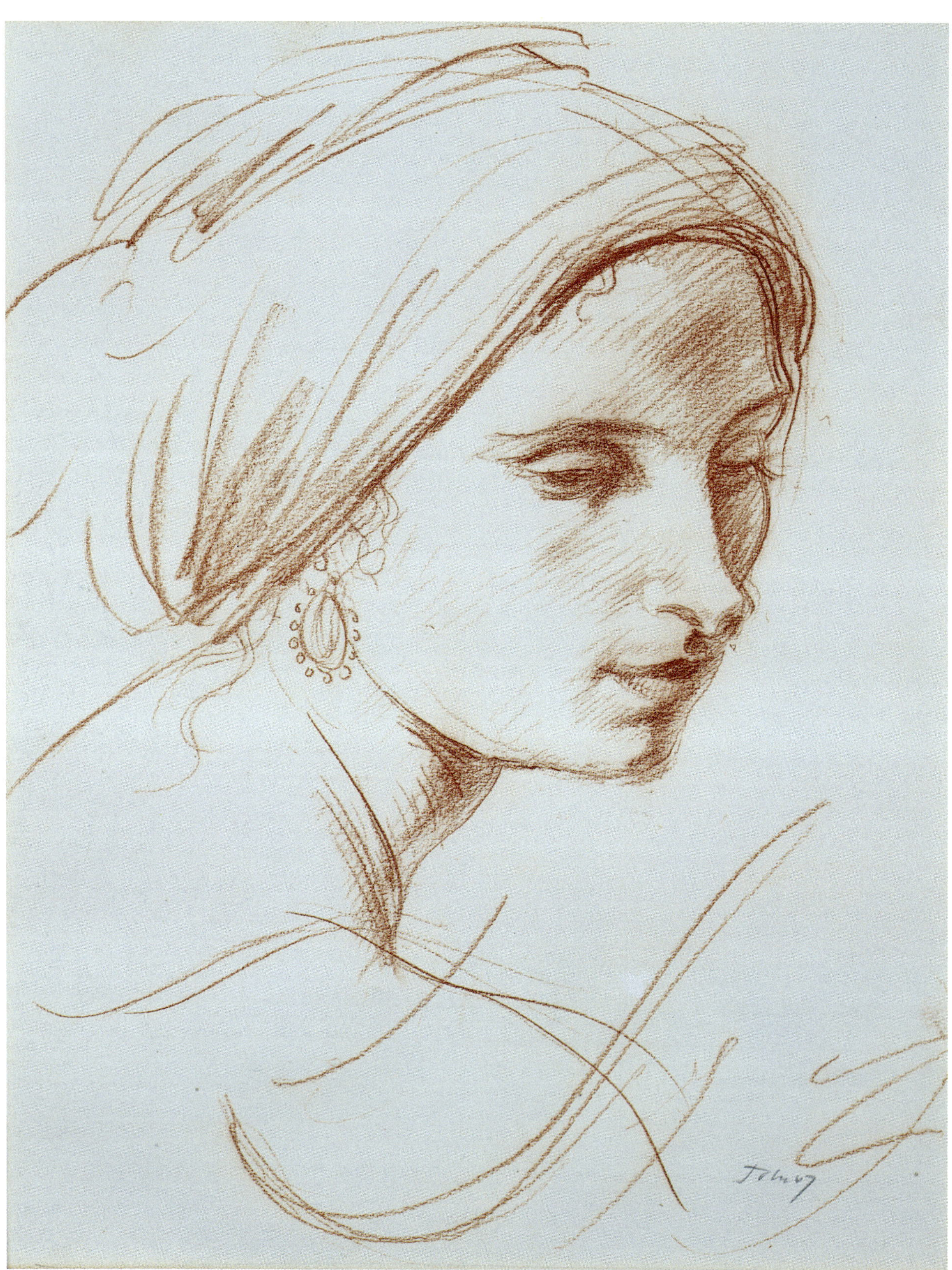

Plate 5
Head of Alick Schepeler,
1906-7, pencil on discoloured greyish white paper (Cat.31)

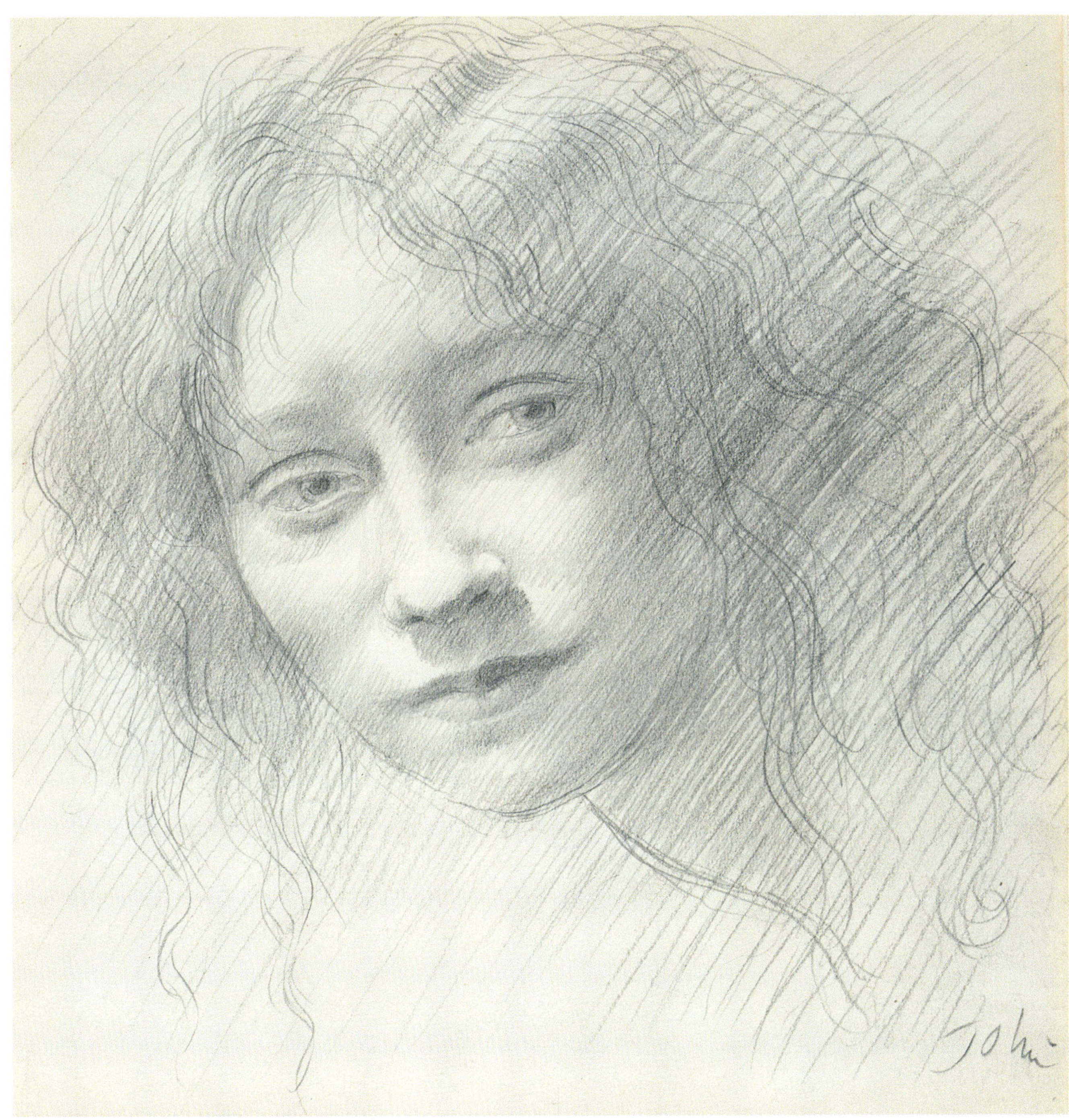

Plate 6
Le Paradou,
1915, ink and wash (Cat.65)

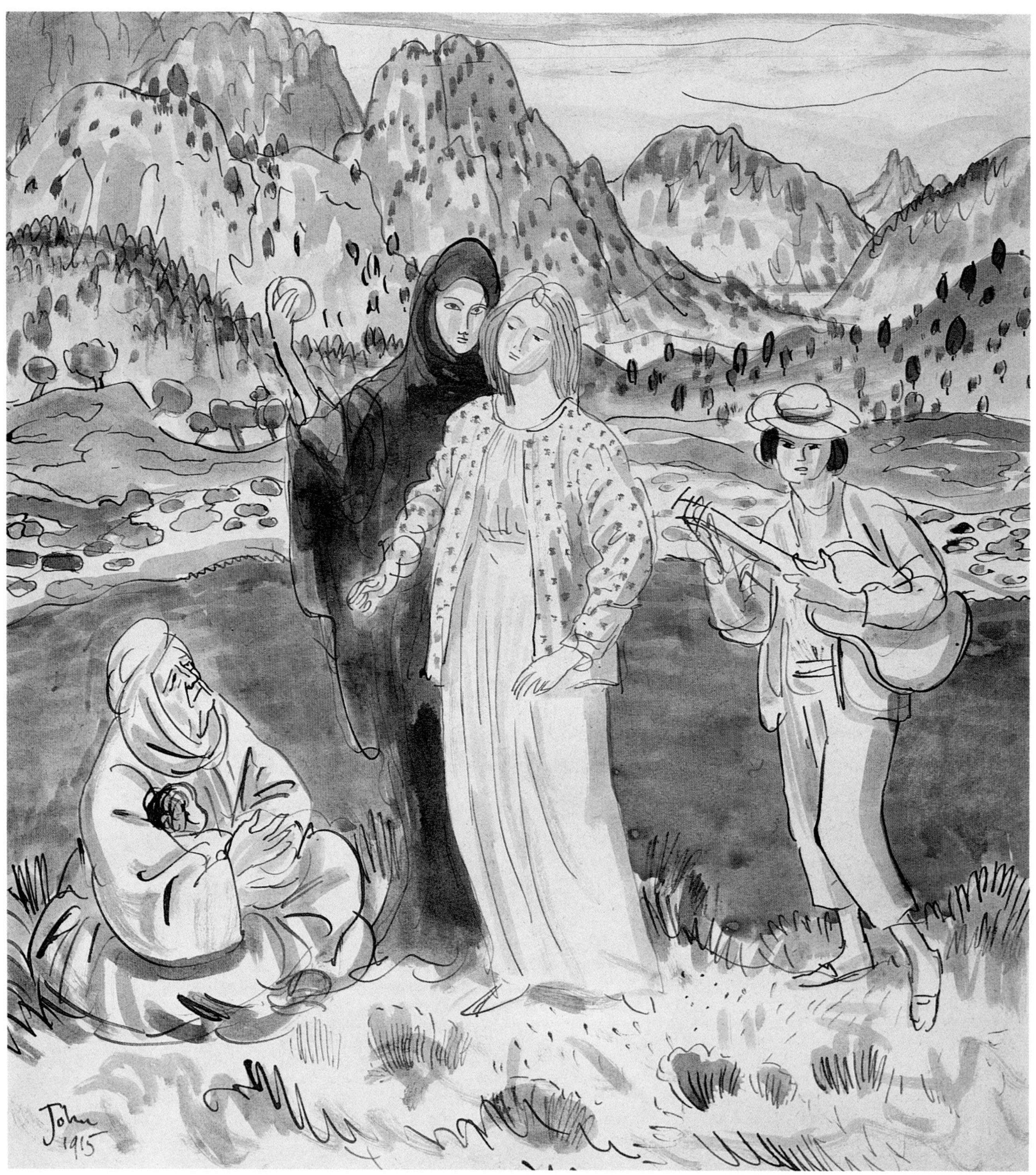

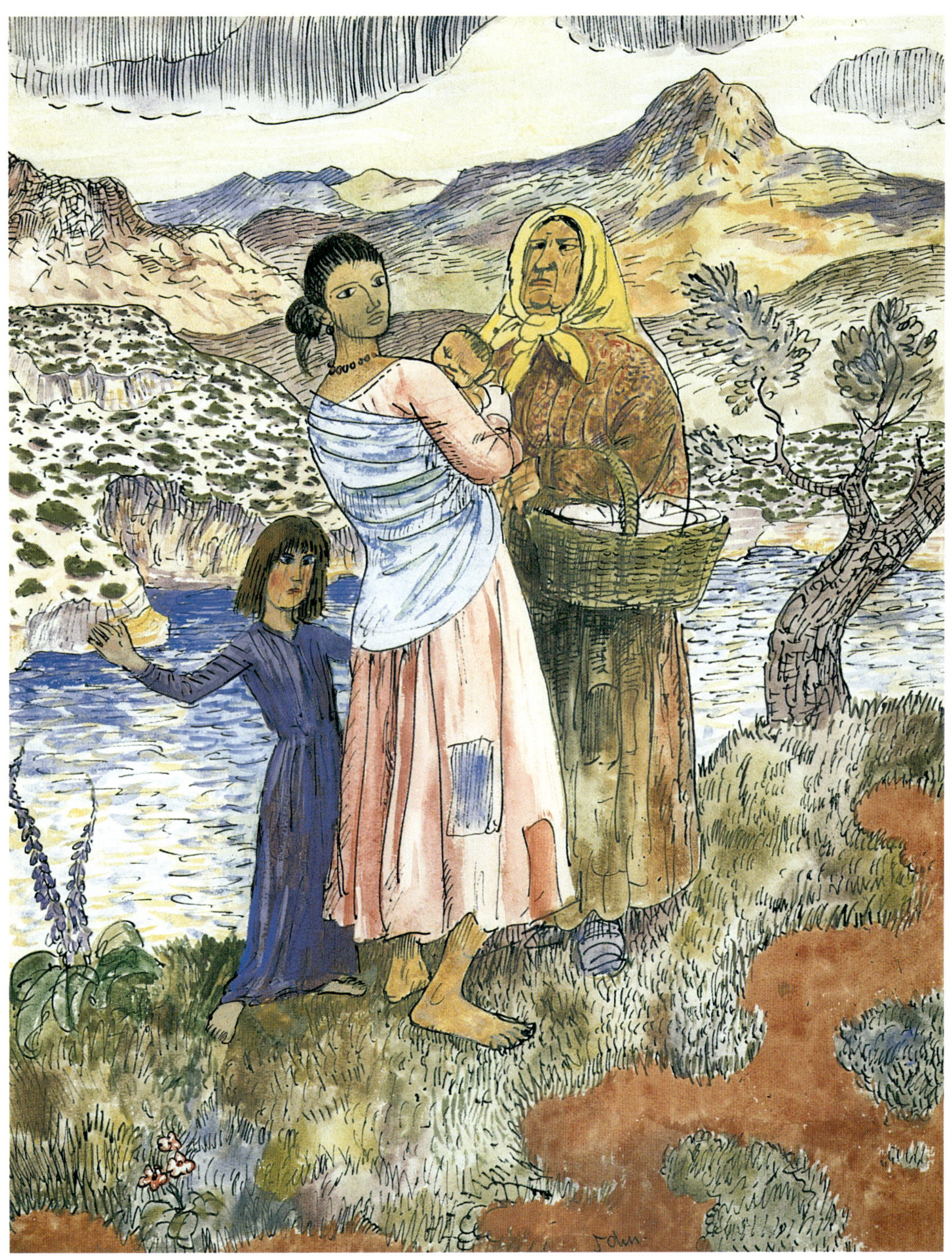

Plate 7
Galway peasants,
1915, ink and watercolour (Cat.67)

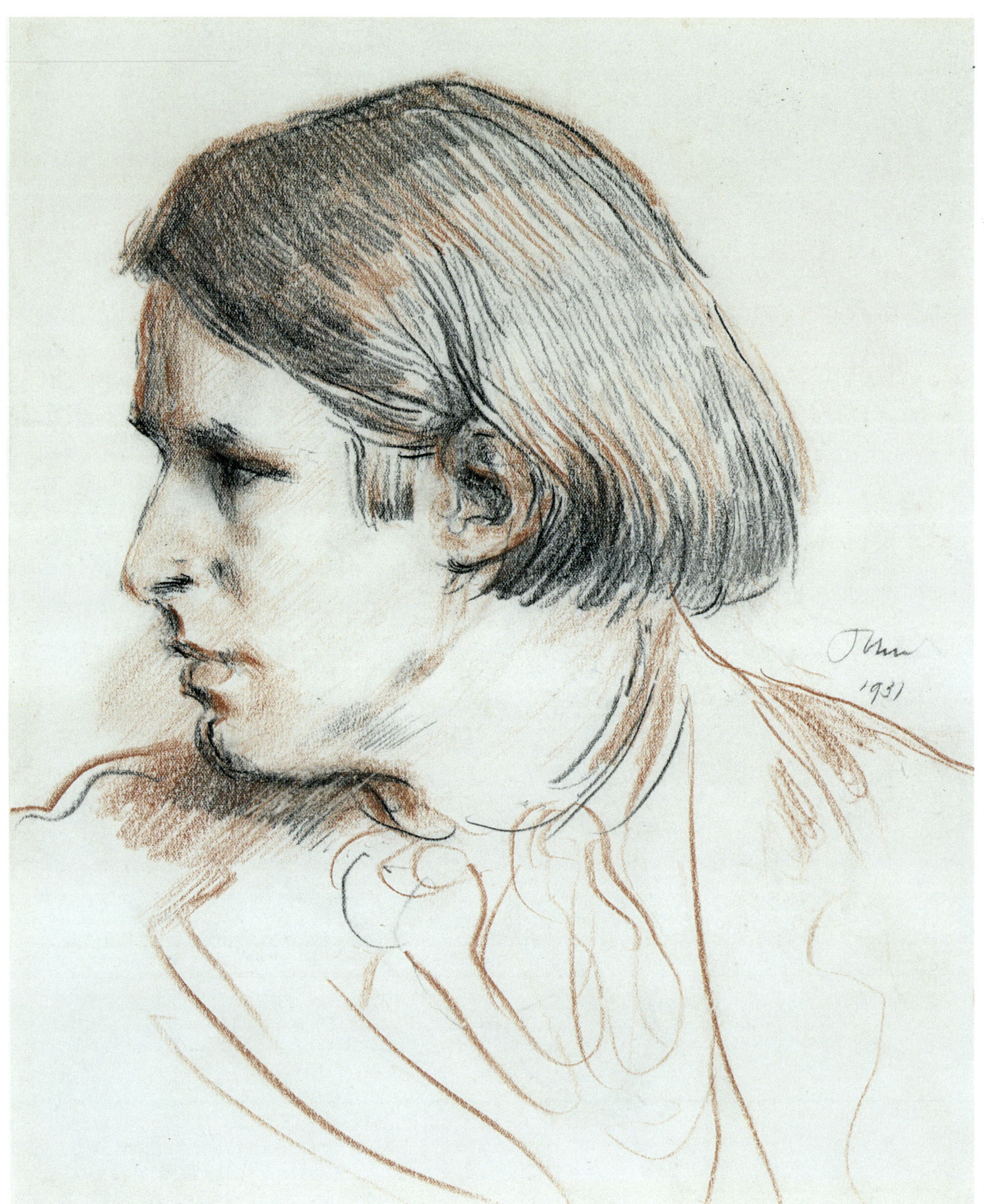

Plate 8
Romilly John,
1931, red and black chalks (Cat.74)

Augustus John and his subjects
Rebecca John

Augustus John drew at great speed, not to race the light, but to catch a moving figure, a turned head, a face in repose. Sometimes he walked around his models; sometimes they moved for him. There are drawings made in rapid succession, others at erratic intervals. 'He worked like a hawk on the wing', a sitter observed in 1909, 'and was white, sweating and exhausted'.[1]

It is now a hundred years since Augustus studied at the Slade School of Art. He left in 1898 and over the ensuing years his principal models comprised a relatively small group of women and children. At the centre were Ida and Dorelia, and their six young sons, David, Caspar, Robin, Edwin, Pyramus and Romilly. For a while, and following the death of Ida in 1907, Dorelia's sister, Edie, came to help with the children. There are numerous drawings too of the enigmatic Alick Schepeler, and the wives of the artists Derwent Lees and Henry Lamb, Edith ('Lyndra') and Euphemia. Further afield, in the wild places of Ireland, Wales and France, he discovered subjects that were to haunt his imagination for life, who crop up repeatedly in his working studies: people encountered on his travels and themselves itinerant: gypsies, mumpers, tramps, refugees; people who made a living in the open; fishergirls, peasants, musicians.

There is a sense of unity to this work, much of it executed in the pursuit of some ideal existence. It was in the 1920s that the demand for commissioned portraits became overwhelming: out went passive beauty, in came a greater psychological involvement with the individual; their personality and facial expression. His work became less spontaneous, more complex.

Three significant events may explain my increasing involvement with my grandfather's legacy: the death of my father, Caspar, in 1984; the day I looked at a 'John' oil and knew instantly that it was not his work; and a morning spent in the Courtauld Institute's Witt Library. A certain book, too, has played its part over the years: Lillian Browse's *Augustus John Drawings*, first published in 1941. There was something about the sequence of drawings that spoke mysteriously to me of rhythm and grace. Those beautiful grey people afloat on their white pages: where had they come from? Why were the girls draped in this way? What was 'Dorelia', whom I had always known as 'Dodo', *doing*, arms held aloft? I would often leaf through this book.

By the time of Caspar's death, I had already become aware of the vast body of work left behind by Augustus. Following his father's death in 1961, Caspar had to devote much time to sorting out the estate (initially while First Sea Lord), a process repeated after Dorelia's death in 1969. He had also to assist with exhibitions, books – principally Michael Holroyd's biography – and answer an erratic stream of enquiries through the post. Could he identify a portrait, authenticate a work? If he felt uncertain about a picture he would pass the query around his brothers and sisters. 'Dear Caper Sauce', brother Edwin replied in May 1975 (another nickname was 'Boatman'), 'I would not hesitate in confirming this to be a portrait of yourself by A E J … To me there can be no doubt at all as to its identity; the 'Chinese' eyes speak for themselves'. (Doubts will remain as to which of his sons Augustus has caught in certain works. It was alleged that he could not tell one from another anyway, and when they grew up, they had much the same difficulty.)

When, at the age of seventy-six, Caspar was confined to a wheelchair, he talked more openly about his responsibilities. I would sometimes sit with him and he would show me what he was doing. Not long after he died, I came one day unexpectedly face to face with a 'John' oil portrait and involuntarily said 'That is not by Augustus'. This was nothing new. Dorelia, among others, had come across similar imitations: 'This morning a bad drawing of Yates [*sic*] attributed to Augustus – Islington Gazette – and a letter with a photograph of a drawing', she informed Caspar in April 1968. 'The owner thought it was by A. and it wasn't. Too many of these drawings about.' This is now an accepted fact, and there have been some recent lamentable examples.

I grew curious and with one eye on works coming on to the market, I began research. This was familiar ground, having worked as a picture researcher, and I was by now anyway thrown back on family history, having taken on my father's biography. I received a few enquiries, and as my visual memory strengthened a new perspective began to form.

In 1987, whilst working on still-life paintings for Elizabeth David in the Witt Library, I decided to take a long look through the 1000 plus photographs of Augustus' work. I had already glanced through this collection on a previous visit, and had been amazed at the number of works I had never seen. This time I began to assemble certain drawings that appeared to belong together. Some had already been documented as such, and David Fraser Jenkins' catalogue for the National Museum of Wales exhibition *Studies for Compositions* (1978) proved an invaluable reference work. To date, this remains the only pictorial record that attempts to analyse the artist's working method and little-known mythological subject-matter, demonstrating how many of his drawings were made as studies, often repeated, with large paintings in mind. But there remained many superb drawings – mainly portraits and single figures – which had clearly been executed within a matter of minutes, and which had never been seen together.

They represented an almost cinematic vision: heads began turning, a figure took a step forward. To take Dorelia: there are over 160 images of her in the Witt today (about 106 drawings, 56 paintings), from which I was able to assemble pairs, trios, quartets. I made further additions by referring to art books, auction and exhibition catalogues, the archives of the National Portrait Gallery and National Museum of Wales, and a small collection of photographs at home.

'Repetition will bring out spiritual qualities', Kandinsky wrote in his book *Concerning the Spiritual in Art* (1912). One thinks of Monet's series paintings, Modigliani's heads, Gwen John's portraits; but in Augustus' case, it was as if in those early years he became supercharged and was unable to stop. He had phenomenal energy, superb eye/hand co-ordination, and since portrait work necessitates repetition – if only to adjust that bump in the nose, redefine that upper lip – we are left with whole series of images of the same model. Conversely, the sense of disappointment commonly felt by artists on completion of a work can spur renewed effort. But there are clear dividing lines between drawings made spontaneously (Ida, Dorelia, the children); studies made as preliminaries for an oil portrait (Suggia); commissioned drawings (Romilly) and working studies for large-scale compositions (Galway peasants). This latter work is more experimental, humorous, and includes work done from memory. And there are those drawings made for small-scale work, such as the etchings.

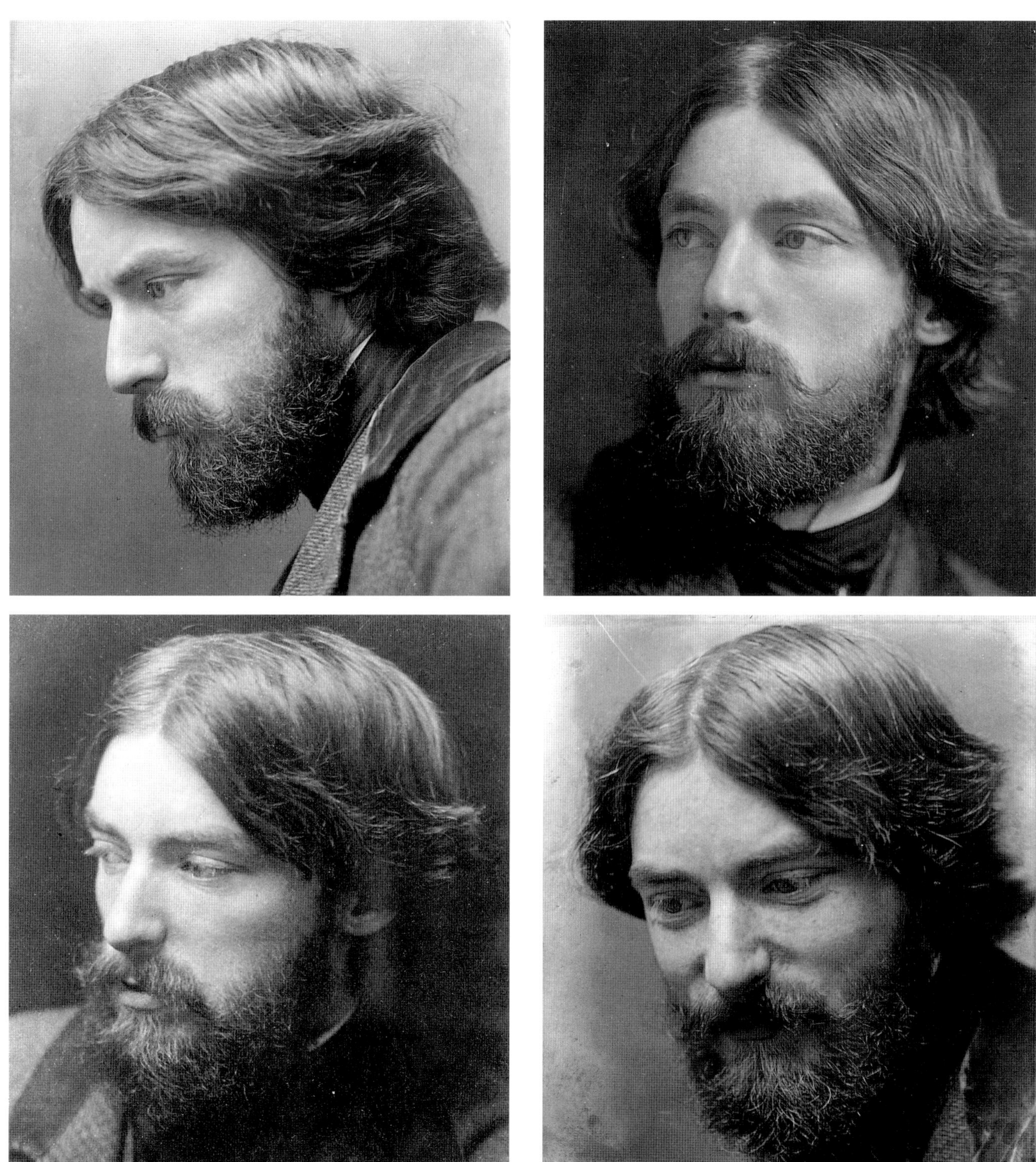

Note

1 Letter from Chaloner Dowdall to Vere Egerton Cotton, 6 November 1945, quoted in Holroyd 1996, p.288. See Select Bibliography on pp.71-2.

Augustus once expressed the view that a portrait only becomes complete on the sitter's death. I think of Tom Stoppard's words from his play *In the Native State* (Faber 1991): 'All portraits should be unfinished otherwise it's like looking at a stopped clock': the drawings assembled for this exhibition appear to be still moving.

Chronology

1878 Born in Tenby, Pembrokeshire

1894-8 Slade School of Fine Art, London

1898 Wins Slade School competition. Visits Holland and Paris

1899 First one-man show. First showing at New English Art Club

1901 Marries Ida Nettleship. Appointed Art Instructor at Liverpool

1902 Son David born. Leaves Liverpool

1903 Meets Dorelia McNeill, who joins *ménage à trois* with Ida until the latter's death. Elected to NEAC. Son Caspar born

1904 Elected to membership of Society of Twelve. Son Robin born

1905 (Dorelia's) son Pyramus born. (Ida's) son Edwin born. Lives in Paris, with frequent returns to London, until 1907

1906 (Dorelia's) son Romilly born

1907 (Ida's) son Henry born. Death of Ida. Visits studio of Picasso. Paints and draws W. B. Yeats in Ireland

1908 Beginning of friendship with Lady Ottoline Morrell

1909 Visits Cambridge and Liverpool, where paints portrait of Lord Mayor

1910 Visits Italy and France. Begins working with J. D. Innes

1911 Elected to Camden Town Group. Moves to Alderney Manor

1912 Visits Ireland, North Wales and France. Death of son Pyramus. Daughter Poppet born

1913 Exhibits at Armory Show, New York. Visits Modigliani in Paris. Included in Cardiff exhibition of *Works by Certain Modern Artists*

1914 Elected President of National Portrait Society

1915 Daughter Vivien born

1916 Major purchase of work by Gwendoline Davies

1917 To France as official artist with Canadian army

1918 Starts Canadian War Cartoon. Included in exhibition organised by Contemporary Arts Society at Zurich

1919 Official artist at Paris Peace Conference. Exhibition of graphic work at Chenil Gallery

1920 Elected Fellow of University College London. *War, Peace Conference and Other Portraits* exhibition at Alpine Club Gallery. Scandal over Lord Leverhulme's portrait

1921 Elected Associate of Royal Academy

1922 Visits Spain

1924 *Mme Suggia* wins first prize at International Exhibition, Pittsburgh

1925 Visits Berlin

1927 Moves from Alderney Manor, Dorset to Fryern Court, Hampshire

1928 Elected Royal Academician

1932 Honorary doctorate from University College, Cardiff

1933 Trustee of Tate Gallery

1934 Elected President of Royal Cambrian Academy

1935 Death of son Henry. Numerous works included in *Contemporary Welsh Art* exhibition

1937 Elected President of Gypsy Lore Society

1938 Represented in Exhibition of British Art at Louvre. Resigns from Royal Academy

1939 Death of Gwen John. Represented at British Council Exhibition, New York

1940 Re-elected to Royal Academy. Honorary Member of the London Group. Retrospective exhibition of drawings at National Gallery

1942 Awarded Order of Merit

1943 Elected Honorary Member, American National Institute of Arts and Letters

1944 Narrowly loses to Alfred Munnings in election for presidency of Royal Academy

1946 Elected member of the Académie Royale de Belgique

1948 Elected President of Royal Society of Portrait Painters

1954 Retrospective exhibition at Royal Academy

1959 Given Honorary Freedom of Tenby

1961 Dies at Fryern Court, Hampshire

1962 First studio sale at Christie's

1963 Second studio sale at Christie's

1967 Memorial statue by Ivor Roberts-Jones at Fordingbridge unveiled

1969 Death of Dorelia

1972 Purchase of remains of studio by National Museum of Wales

1974 Retrospective exhibition of early prints and drawings at Colnaghi's, London

1975 Retrospective exhibition of paintings and drawings, National Portrait Gallery

1978 Centenary exhibitions at Cambridge, Cardiff, Sheffield and New Haven, USA

Catalogue

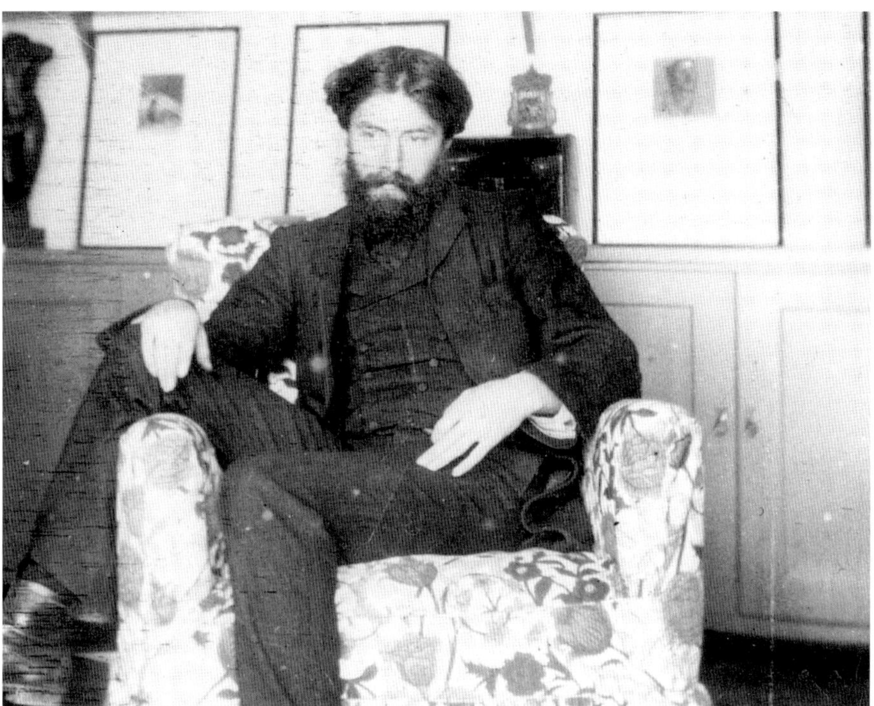

Augustus John, *c.*1900

In the introduction to the National Gallery's exhibition of his drawings in 1940, John wrote: 'It has been impossible to trace some drawings I would like to have included, while other typical examples have proved unavailable'. Fifty-six years later, this statement still applies, and three key works which have proved untraceable are represented by illustrations in the catalogue. The works are grouped thematically and broadly chronologically. Abbreviated bibliographic references are to works listed in the Select Bibliography on pp.71-2.

Omar Khayyam, 1901

These studies were made for the frontispiece to John Sampson's Romany version of Edward Fitzgerald's translation of the *Rubaiyat of Omar Khayyam* published by David Nutt in 1902. Sampson was a friend of the artist, Librarian at the University of Liverpool and a specialist in Romany, the language of gypsies. Both illustrate a recurrent theme in the *Rubaiyat*, throughout which the 'Beloved' is repeatedly invited to 'Fill the Cup!' and live for the day, while being warned of life's transience. Four pen and ink studies are known, two of which depict the man in a turban. He was portrayed in the frontispiece version as a gypsy (Cat.2), a more appropriate *persona* for this Romany 'rendering'. This also shows a less scantily clad girl, and is signed JANIK, Romany for *John.*

1 *The Rubaiyat of Omar Khayyam*
ink and wash, 37×29.1 cm ($7\frac{5}{8} \times 10\frac{1}{4}$ in)
PROV: Purchased from the Redfern Gallery
Private Collection

2 *Omar*
ink and wash on buff paper,
37×29.1 cm ($14\frac{1}{2} \times 11\frac{1}{2}$ in)
Signed: JANIK (bottom left)
LIT: Rothenstein 1944, p.8 and no.86;
exh. Cardiff 1978, no.21
PROV: Sir Michael Sadler
Lent by the Trustees of the Cecil Higgins
Art Gallery, Bedford (Inv.P394)
[Exhibited in Cardiff only]

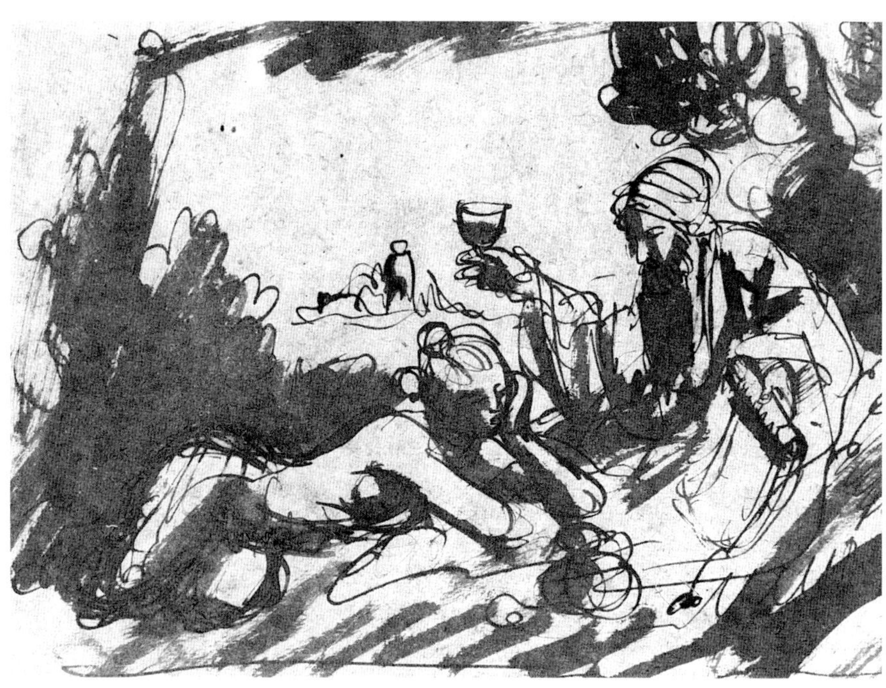

1

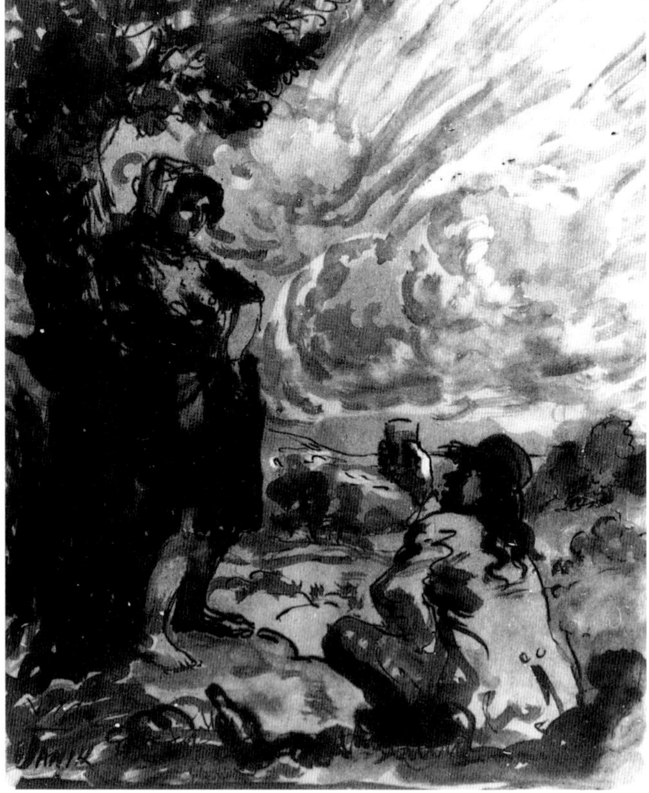

2

Benjamin Waugh, *c.*1901-6

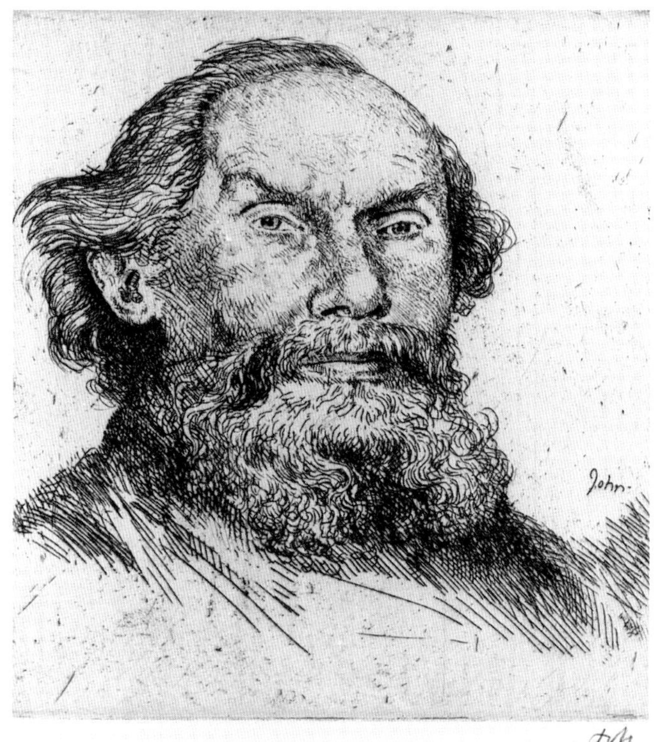

4

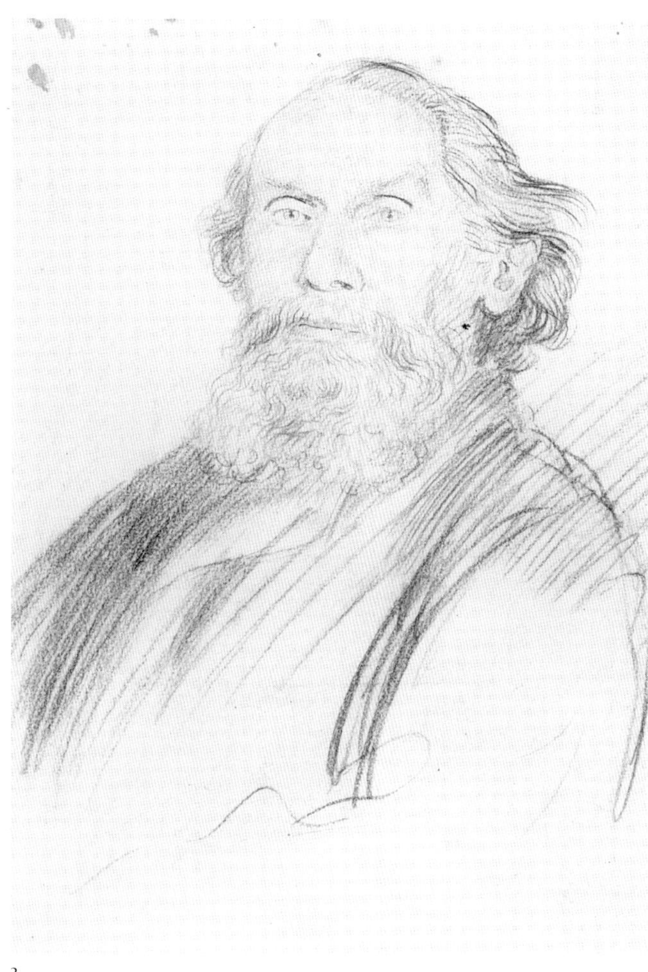

3

The congregationalist minister Benjamin Waugh (1839-1908) was editor of the *Sunday Magazine* and the founder of the NSPCC in 1889. The same year he was responsible for 'The Children's Charter', Parliament's first Act for the Prevention of Cruelty to Children. In 1873 he wrote and published anonymously *The Gaol Cradle – Who Rocks It?* on the fate of young offenders. John met him through his friendship with Waugh's daughter, Edna Clark Hall, a contemporary at the Slade. This delicate pencil study, which is mirrored in the smaller etching, first published in 1906, was done when Waugh was near the end of his life, exhausted from almost forty years of campaigning for children's rights.

3 *Bust of Benjamin Waugh*
pencil, 35.5×25.4 cm (14×10 in)
Lent by Mrs R. MacDonald Hall

4 *Head of Benjamin Waugh*
etching, 16.2×14.9 cm (6½×5⅞ in)
Incised: *John* (two thirds down, right, in the plate)
Signed: *John* (in pencil, bottom right, below plate)
LIT: Campbell Dodgson 1920, no.23; exh. Cardiff 1988, no.7
PROV: Presented by the artist, 1920
National Museum and Gallery, Cardiff
(NMW A 3487)

Ida John, standing, *c.*1902-6

The model is the artist's first wife Ida,
the daughter of the animal painter John
Trivett Nettleship (1841-1902), who
arrived at the Slade in 1892 and married
John in January 1901. Three of these
drawings have been exhibited
periodically, and are assembled here with
a previously unknown version on blue
paper. At least six other variations of Ida
in this costume are known. The dress,
with its torn armpit, is untypical of Ida
(who was meticulous about her clothes),
and she is portrayed not as the woman
who tried so hard to come to terms with
her role as a wife, but as the artist's
model. Cat.8 was used in the large oil
painting *The way down to the sea* (private
collection), exhibited in 1909 and at the
Armory Show in 1913 (see Cats 45-7).

5 *Ida in a large hat*
pencil, 29.8×22.8 cm (11¾×9 in)
Signed: *John* (centre, right)
LIT: exh. London 1948, no.64; London
1954, no.20; London 1974, no.53
PROV: Purchased from the artist
Collection of the late Morton H. Sands

6 *Ida, study for 'The way down to the sea'*
charcoal, 61×46.5 cm (24¾×18¼ in)
Signed: *John* (bottom right)
LIT: exh. London 1974, no.48
PROV: Sir Caspar John; Lady John
Private Collection

7 *Ida, study for 'The way down to the sea'*
pencil on blue paper, 50.4×32.6 cm
(17¼×10⅜ in)
PROV: Claude Adams
Lent by John Adams

8 *Ida, study for 'The way down to the sea'*
pencil on discoloured greyish white
paper, 50.4×32.6 cm (19⅞×12⅞ in)
LIT: exh. London 1974, no.52; Cambridge
1978, no.49; Cardiff 1978, no.86
PROV: Chenil Gallery; Dr Louis
C. G. Clarke; by whom bequeathed, 1961
Lent by the Syndics of the Fitzwilliam
Museum, Cambridge (PD.159-1961)

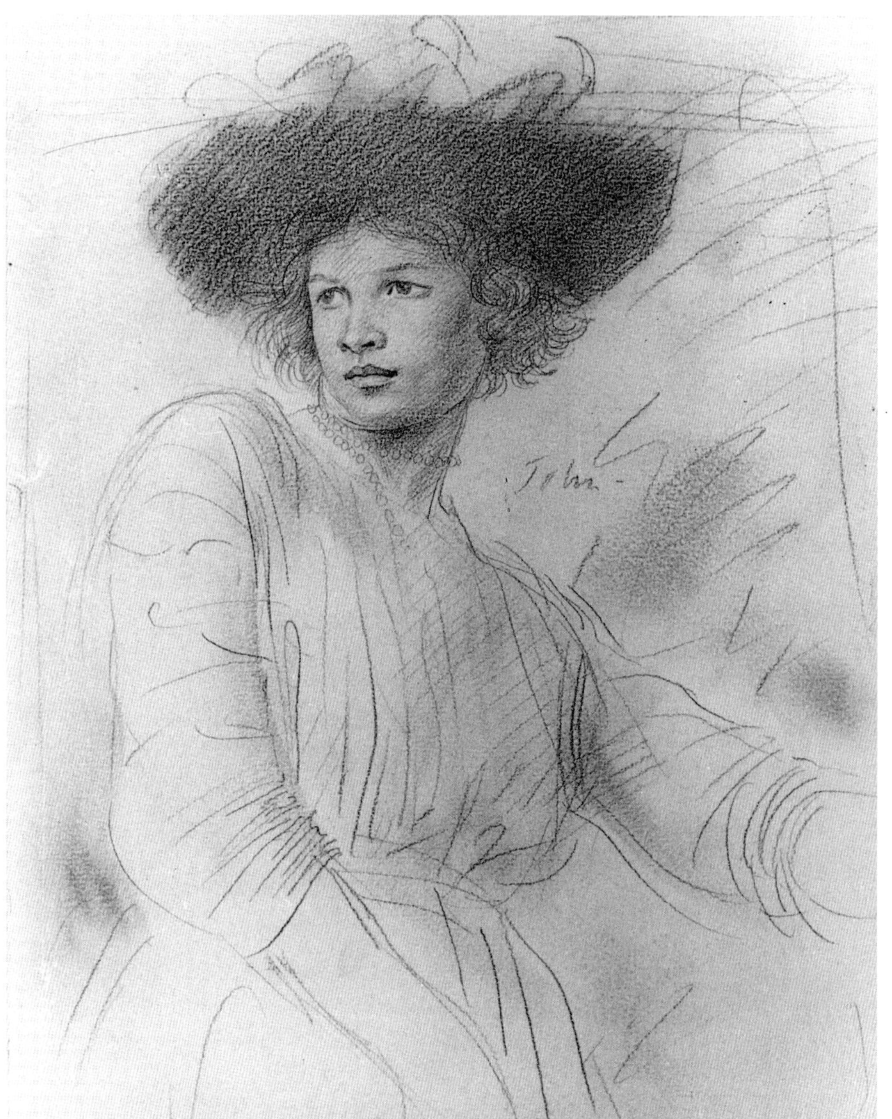

5

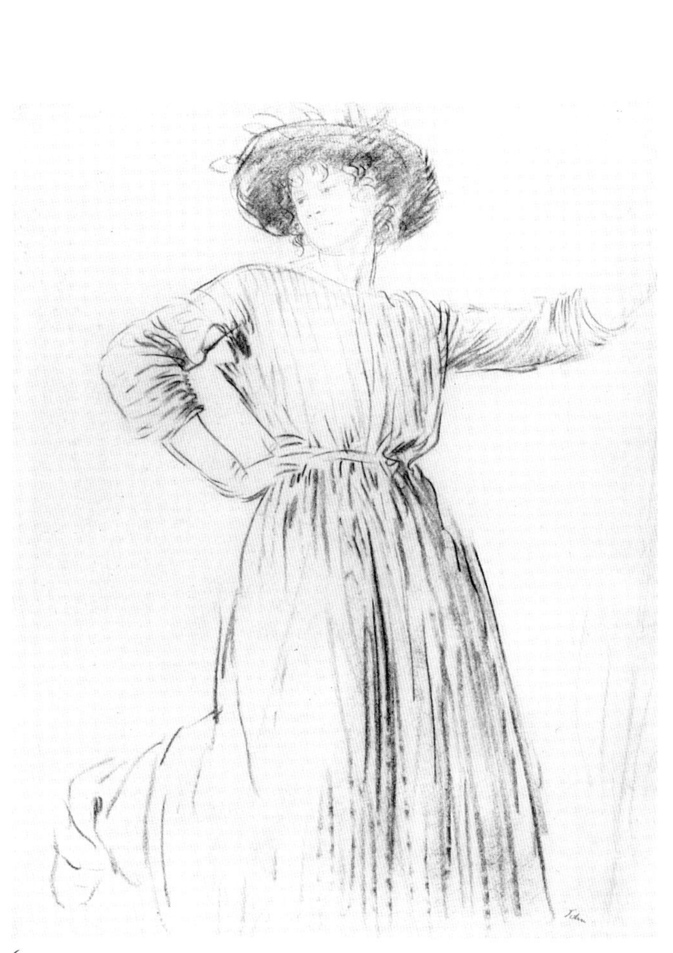

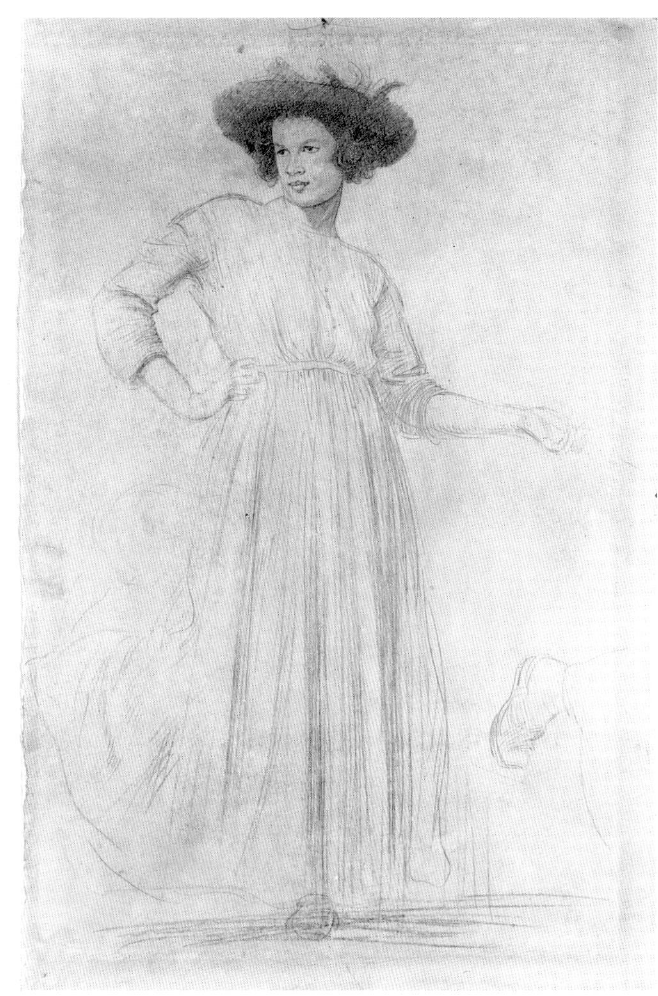

6

8

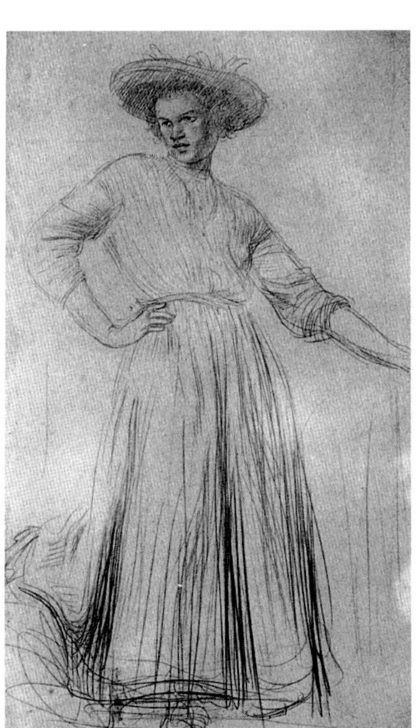

7 (Colour plate 1)

Dorelia McNeill, 1903

John first met Dorelia McNeill early in 1903 and from 1904-7 she lived with Augustus and Ida. These portraits are among the earliest known of Dorelia, and they are certainly some of the most powerful. In Cat.10 (first exhibited in November 1903) her expression is caught in nuance, the fainter image unintentionally animating the stronger, while Cat.9 and a closely related work (Fig.1, private collection) portray the face of uncompromising beauty. Holroyd writes (1996, p.129): 'It was not by her looks alone that she dazzled him. Beauty is not so scarce. What was uncommon about Dorelia was the serenity that gave her beauty its depth … She was not witty or articulate; and certainly not sentimental.'

9 *Study of Dorelia, head and shoulders*
red and black chalk on pale grey paper,
32.4×23.5 cm (12¾×9¼ in)
Signed: *A.E.John* (bottom right)
PROV: Leicester Galleries; Spink & Son
Private Collection, c/o Spink & Son

10 *Miss McNeill (Dorelia)*
black chalk, 37.8×29.4 cm (14⅞×11½ in)
PROV: Charles L. Rutherston; by whom presented, 1925
Lent by Manchester City Art Galleries (1925.368)

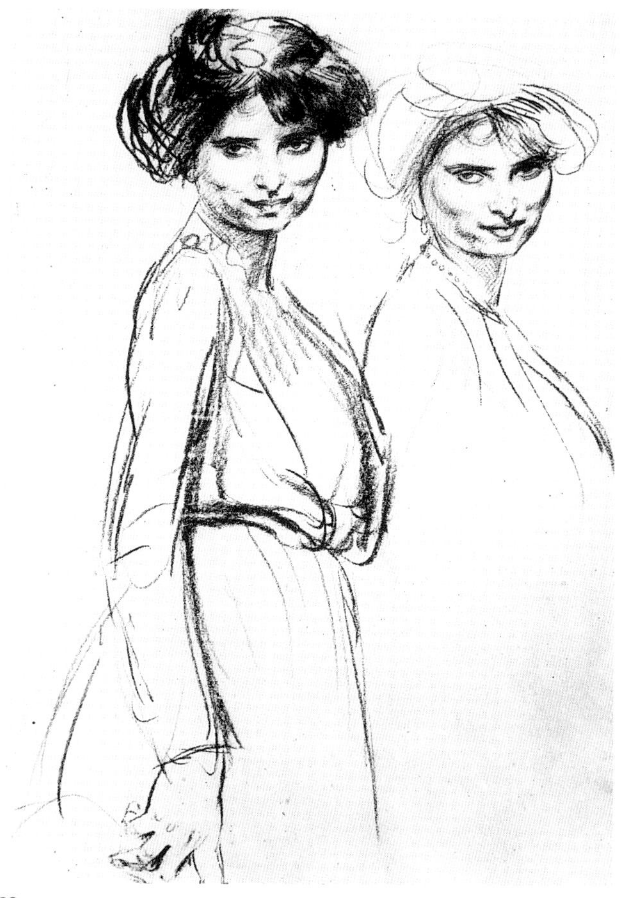

10

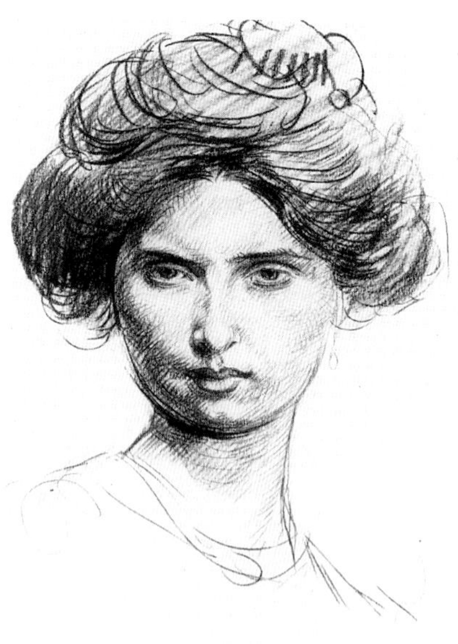

9 (Colour plate 2)

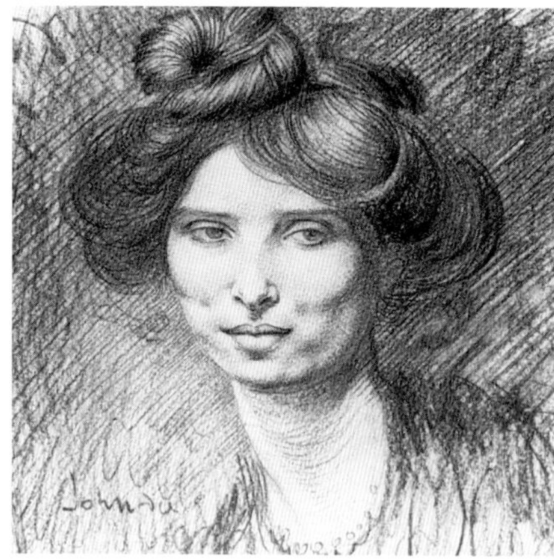

Fig.1 *Head of Dorelia*, black chalk, private collection

Dorelia McNeill, *c.*1903-6

This portrait has the heart-shaped face of
Dorelia as seen by Gwen John in her oil
portraits of 1903. The hairstyle with
plaits gives the sitter a more girlish look,
and she is positively compacted in the
etching. John also produced a rather
larger etching of a similar portrait
(9.9×8.1 cm; Campbell Dodgson, no.54),
which only exists in a single signed
impression and a handful of cancelled
impressions. The rare first state of Cat.12,
was much larger (20×12.5 cm), and
depicted the rest of the figure, draped in
a shawl, lightly sketched. All but the
head and neck was subsequently effaced,
and the plate cut on all sides except the
top to the present size.

11 *Dorelia McNeill*
black chalk, 35.4×25.2 cm (14×10 in)
Signed: *John* (lower right)
LIT: exh. Cardiff 1988, no.11
PROV: Bequeathed by Duncan
T. Norman, 1974
National Museum and Gallery, Cardiff
(NMW A 1859)

12 *Girl in a shawl (Dorelia)*
etching, 8.4×7 cm ($3\frac{5}{8}×2\frac{3}{4}$ in)
Signed: *John* (in pencil, bottom right,
below plate)
LIT: Campbell Dodgson 1920, no.51,
state III
PROV: Presented by the artist, 1920
National Museum and Gallery, Cardiff
(NMW A3669)

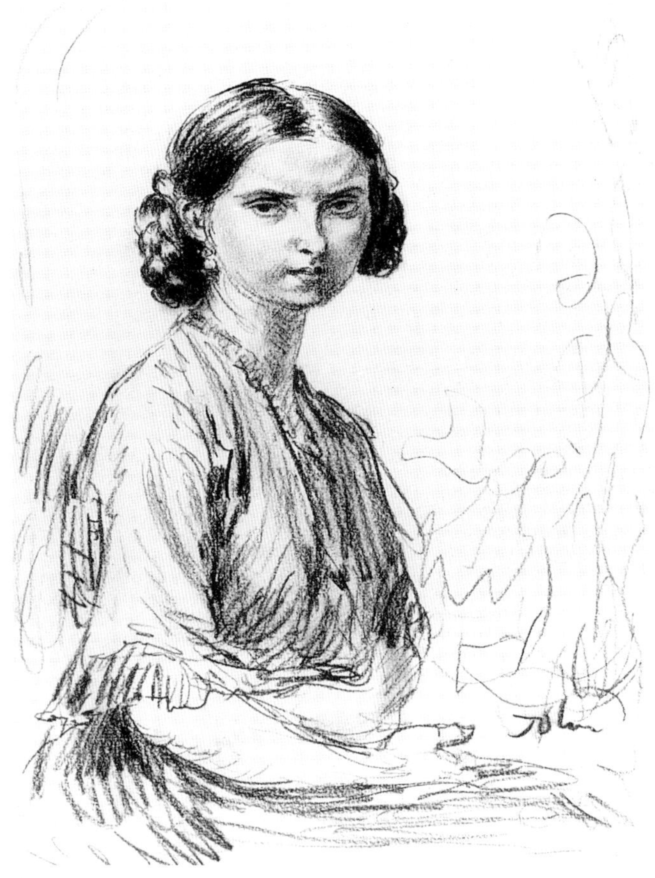

11

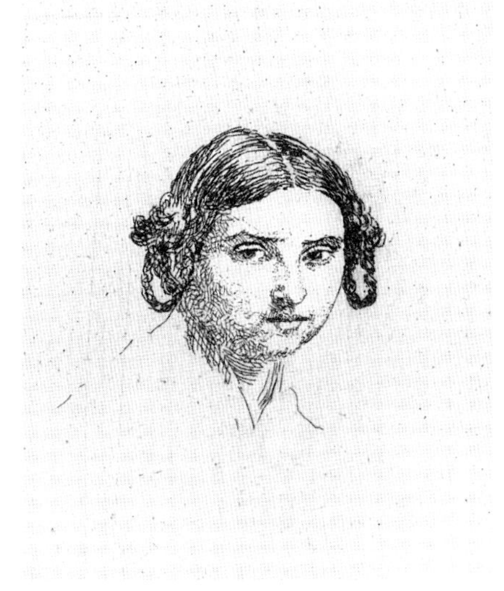

12

Dorelia wearing a hat, *c.*1904-6

John depicted Dorelia in a wide variety
of headgear, including several broad-
brimmed hats. This pair of drawings
belongs to a sequence of at least five
(Fig.2, private collection). The hat
suggests the outdoors, and she has the
unwashed look of someone who has
spent the night in the open. The
flickering lines around the figure animate
the whole series, and are indicative of
the speed at which the drawings were
made.

13 *Dorelia wearing a hat*
dark red chalk, 35.5×25.3 cm (14×10 in)
Signed: *John* (in arabesque, bottom right)
LIT: exh. London 1974, no.64;
Cambridge 1978, no.72
PROV: Chenil Gallery; Dr Louis
C. G. Clarke; by whom bequeathed, 1961
Lent by the Syndics of the Fitzwilliam
Museum, Cambridge (PD.159-1961)

14 *Dorelia McNeill wearing a hat*
dark red chalk, 35.5×25.3 cm (14×10 in)
Signed: *John* (bottom left)
PROV: William Rothenstein; by whom
presented, 1912
Lent by Cartwright Hall, Bradford Art
Galleries and Museums (Inv. 1912-041)

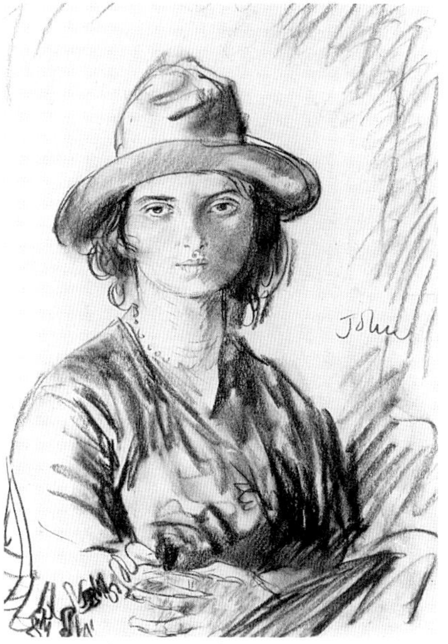

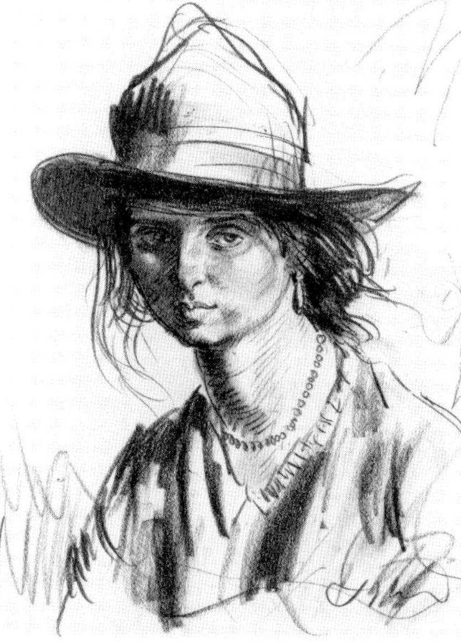

Fig.2 *Dorelia wearing a hat*, charcoal, private
collection

13 (Colour plate 3)

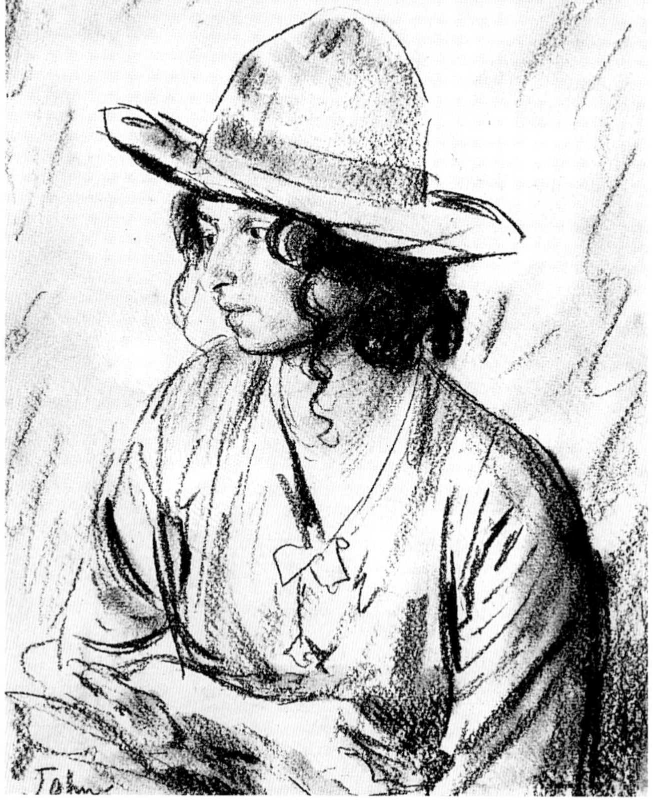

14

Self-portraits, *c.*1901-6

John took up etching in Liverpool in 1901 and produced at least ten self-portrait etchings, mainly in full face. The most celebrated of these, *Tête farouche* ('Head of a wild man' Cat.17) was inspired by Rembrandt's etched *Self-portrait* of 1630 and expresses a self-consciously 'Bohemian' character. These self-portraits almost certainly post-date the accident described by Ida John in a letter to her mother in October 1901: 'Gus has broken his nose and put his finger out of joint by falling from a ladder in the studio. The doctor came – a splendid big red-brown man – and sewed up the cut on the nose in two exquisite stitches. Poor Gus was very white, and bloody in parts. He is now a lovely sight, very much swollen and one little tiny red eye. His profile is like a lion. They say the scar will not show and he will be well in a fortnight. The bone was a little damaged, but it won't make any difference – we think his nose may be straighter after!' (Holroyd 1996, pp.109-10).

15 *Portrait of the artist: in a black gown*
etching, 16.3×9.6 cm ($6\frac{3}{8}$×$3\frac{7}{8}$ in)
Incised: *John* (top right, in the plate)
Signed: *Aug. E. John* (in pencil, bottom right, below plate)
LIT: Campbell Dodgson 1920, no.7, state IV
PROV: Presented by the artist, 1920
National Museum and Gallery, Cardiff
(NMW A3671)

16 *Portrait of the artist: bust, in an oval*
etching, 12.5×10 cm (5×4 in)
Signed: *Aug. E. John* (in pencil, bottom right, below plate)
LIT: Campbell Dodgson 1920, no.9, state III
PROV: Presented by the artist, 1920
National Museum and Gallery, Cardiff
(NMW A3670)

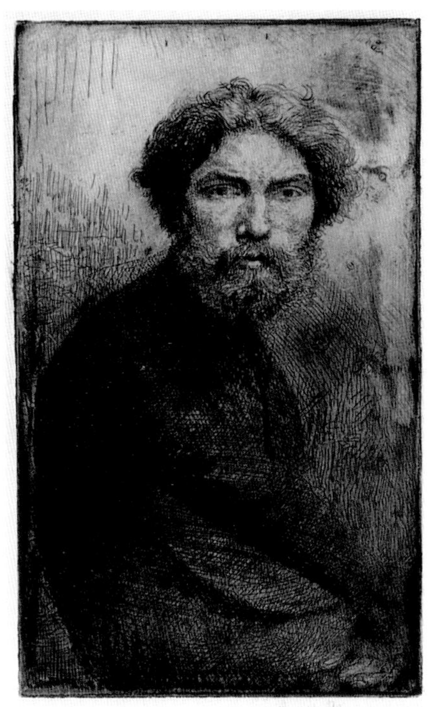

15

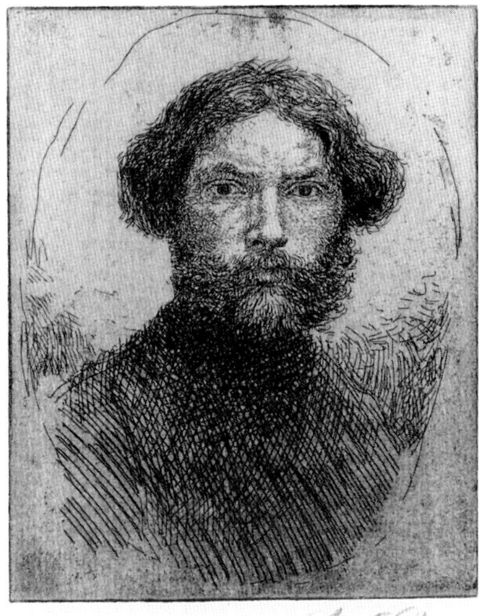

16

17 *Portrait of the artist: 'Tête farouche'*
etching, 21.3×16.9 cm ($8\frac{3}{8}$×$6\frac{5}{8}$ in)
Signed: *Aug. E. John* (in pencil, right, below plate)
LIT: Campbell Dodgson 1920, no.10, state II; Easton and Holroyd 1974, no.29; exh. Cardiff 1988, no.2
PROV: Presented by the artist, 1920
National Museum and Gallery, Cardiff
(NMW A3480)

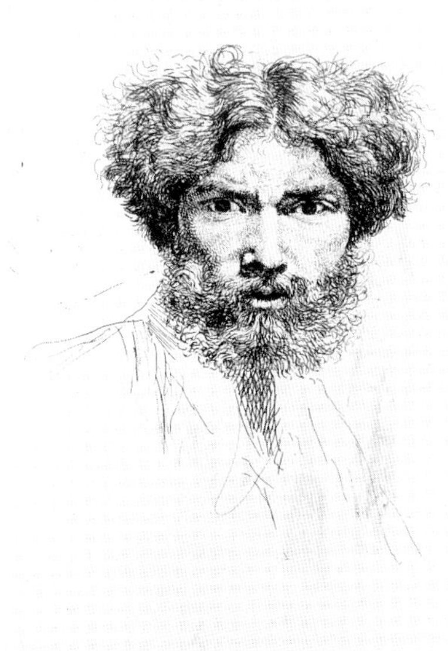

17

Ida and Dorelia, *c.*1905

These red chalk drawings portray the
unconventional friendship between the
two sitters which is best brought to life
by the letter Ida wrote to Dorelia in
1905 about their roles in the *ménage à
trois* that they had formed with John the
previous year:
'A woman is either a wife or a mistress. If
a wife, she has (that is, her position
implies) perfect confidence in her
husband and peace of mind – not being
concerned about any other woman in
relation to her husband. But she has ties
and responsibility and is, more or less, a
fixture – and not free. If a mistress she
has no right to expect faithfulness, and
must allow a man to come and go as he
will without question – and must in
consequence, if she loves him jealously,
suffer doubt and not have peace of mind
– *but* she has her own freedom too. Well
here are you and I – we have neither the
peace of mind of the wife nor the
freedom (at least I haven't) of the
mistress. We have the evils of both states
for the one good, which belongs to both
– a man's company. Is it worth it? Isn't it
paying twice over for our boon?

Our only remedy is to both become
mistresses, and so at any rate have the
privileges of the mistress.

Of course I have the children and
perhaps, being able to avail myself of the
name of wife, I ought to do so, and live
with G[us]. But I shall never consider
myself as a wife – it is a mockery'
(Holroyd 1996, p.185).

18 *Ida Nettleship and Dorelia McNeill*
red chalk, 24.7×34.9 cm (9¾×13¾ in)
Signed: *John* (top right)
LIT: exh. London 1940, no.101; London
1948, no.110; London 1965, no.1.
Lent by Her Majesty Queen Elizabeth
The Queen Mother

18a *Ida Nettleship and Dorelia McNeill*
red chalk, 29.2×23.5 cm (11½×9¼ in)
PROV: Sold Christie's 19 July 1968, lot
78; Thomas Agnew & Sons
Private Collection

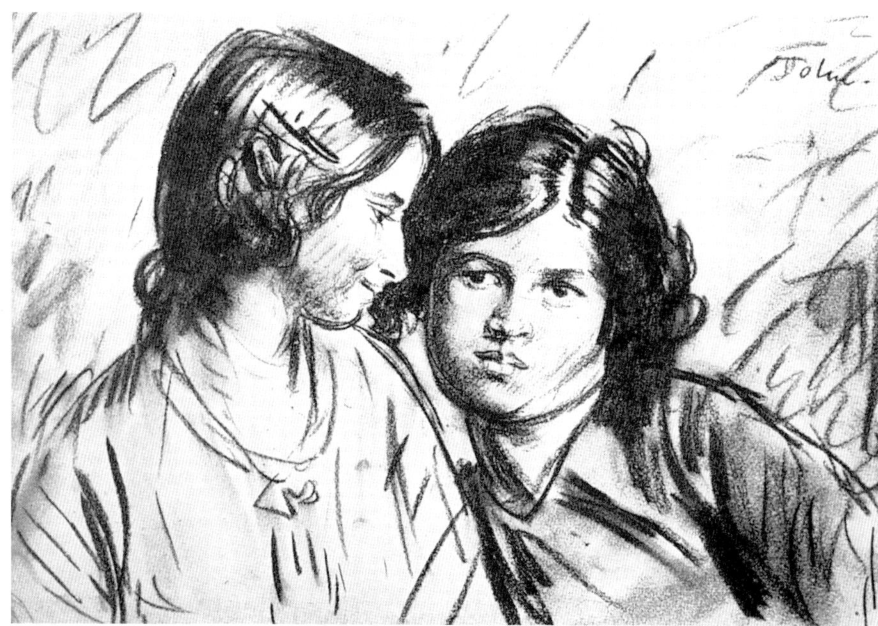
18 (Ida is the right-hand figure in both drawings)

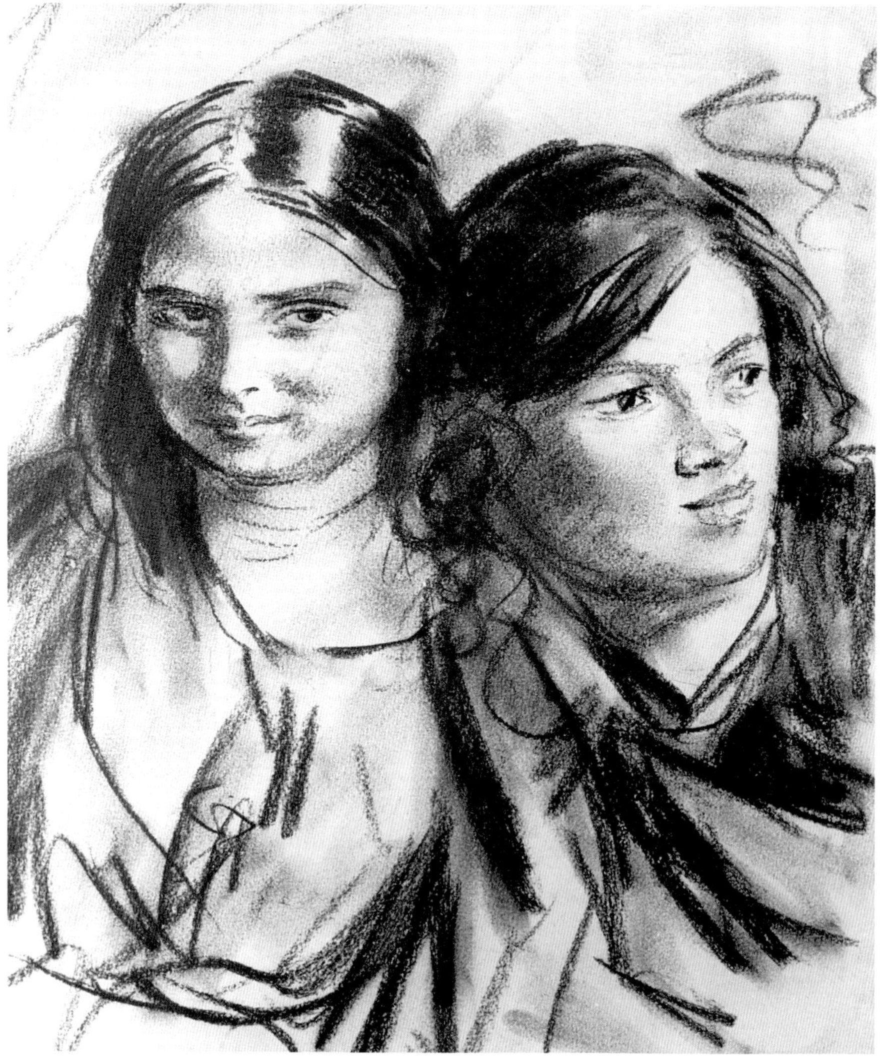
18A

Jacob Epstein, *c.*1905-6

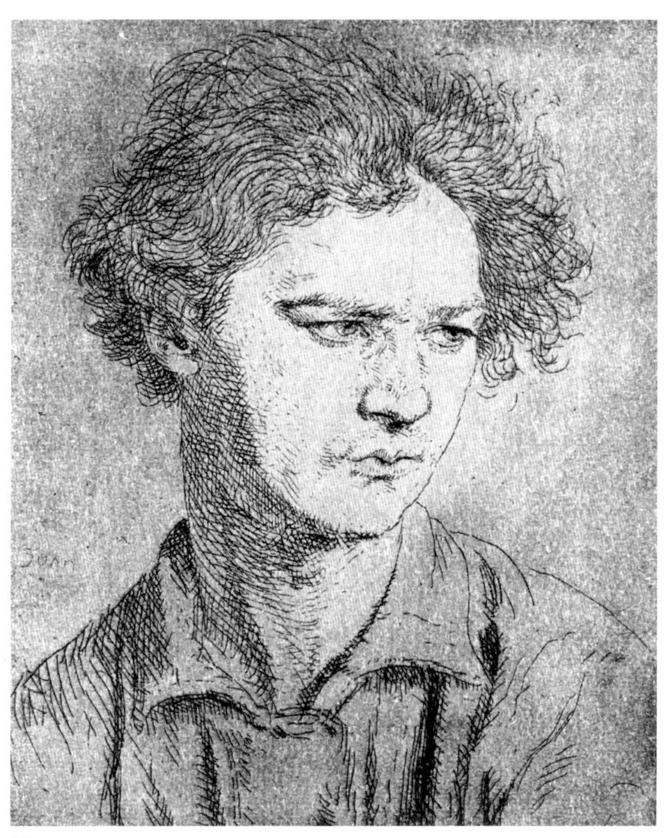

20

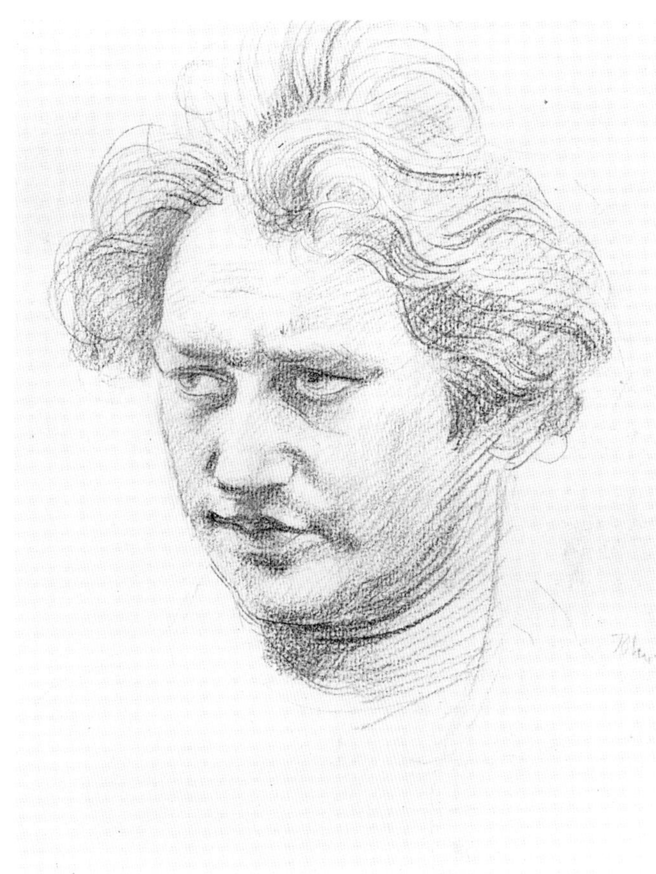

19

In 1905 the American sculptor Jacob Epstein (1880-1959) moved from Paris to London, where he soon became acquainted with John and other members of the New English Art Club. John produced several drawings of Epstein and two etchings, one at full face (Campbell Dodgson, no.13). In 1907 Epstein executed a bronze head of the painter's son Romilly, followed in 1910 by the stone version in the National Museum and Gallery, Cardiff (NMW A2532) and in 1916 by a bronze head of Augustus. Although they encouraged each other, the two artists had a prickly friendship, which animated their portraits of one another.

19 *Jacob Epstein*
black chalk, 27.3×19.4 cm (10¾×7⅝ in)
Signed: *John* (lower right)
LIT: Longstreet 1967, p.25
PROV: Given by the National Art-Collections Fund, 1959
Lent by the National Portrait Gallery, London (4119)

20 *Jacob Epstein, sculptor. No.1*
etching, 12.5×10 cm (5×3⅞ in)
Incised: *John* (two thirds down, left, in the plate)
Signed: *John* (in pencil, bottom right, below plate)
LIT: Campbell Dodgson 1920, no.12; exh. Cardiff 1988, no.13
PROV: Presented by the artist, 1920
National Museum and Gallery, Cardiff (NMW A3470)

Fruit sellers, 1901-6

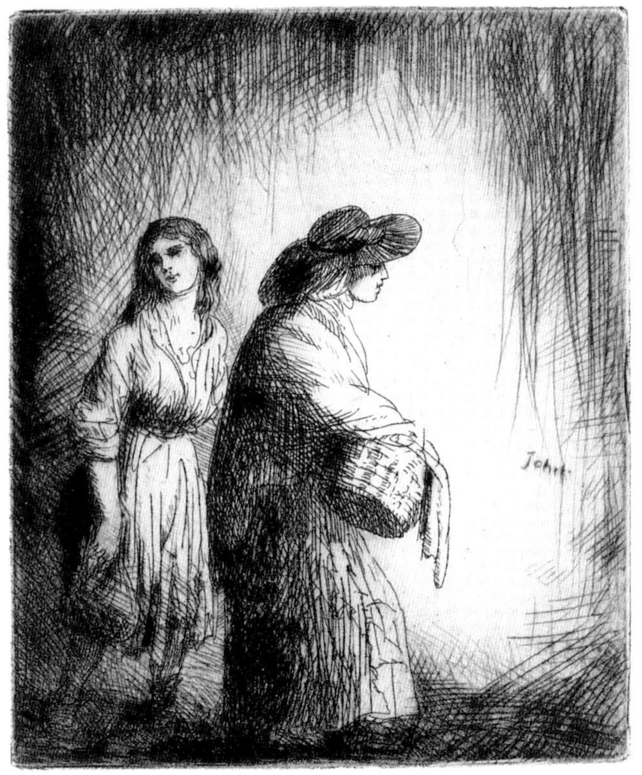

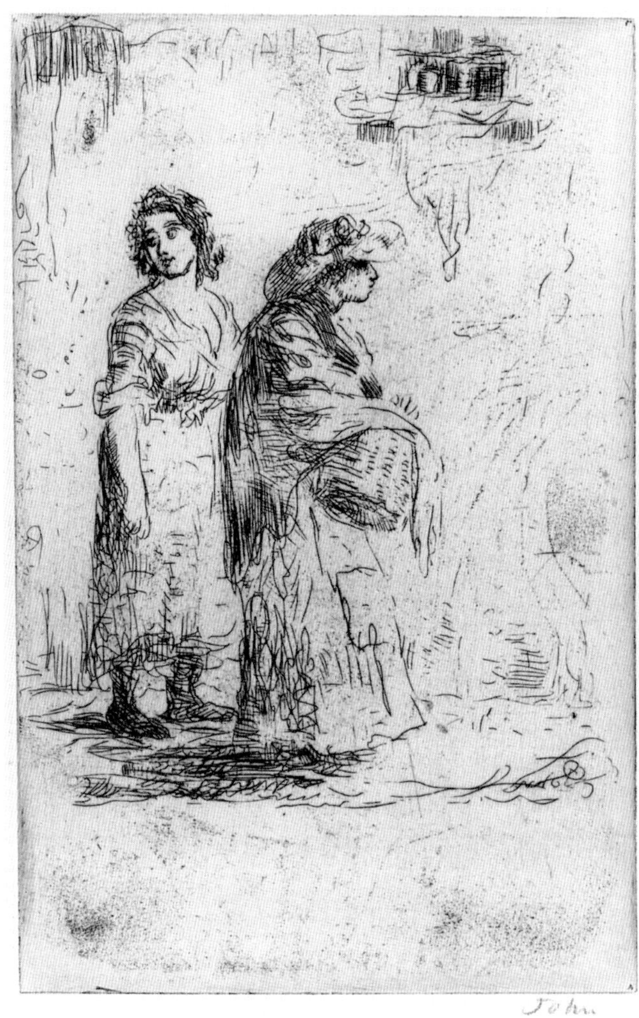

21

22

John produced five different etched versions of this composition (Campbell Dodgson, nos 86-90), of which the first four were published in 1906, and the last in 1919. Its subject-matter recalls earlier etchings of urban working-class life by Rembrandt and Whistler. John's sources are especially clear in Cat.21, which employs dramatic lighting effects derived from Rembrandt, and Cat.22, which has a broken, impressionistic technique reminiscent of Whistler.

21 *Fruit sellers – C.*
etching and drypoint, 11.6 × 9.5 cm (4½ × 3¾ in)
Incised: *John* (two thirds down, right, in the plate)
Signed: *A. E. John* (in pencil, bottom right, below plate)
LIT: Campbell Dodgson 1920, no.88, state IV
PROV: Presented by the artist, 1920
National Museum and Gallery, Cardiff (NMW A3668)

22 *Fruit sellers – E.*
etching, 20.3 × 12.7 cm (8 × 5 in)
Incised: *John* (indistinct and in reverse, lower right, in the plate)
Signed: *John* (in pencil, bottom right, below plate)
LIT: Campbell Dodgson 1920, no.90
PROV: Presented by the artist, 1920
National Museum and Gallery, Cardiff (NMW A3667)

Caspar John, 1906

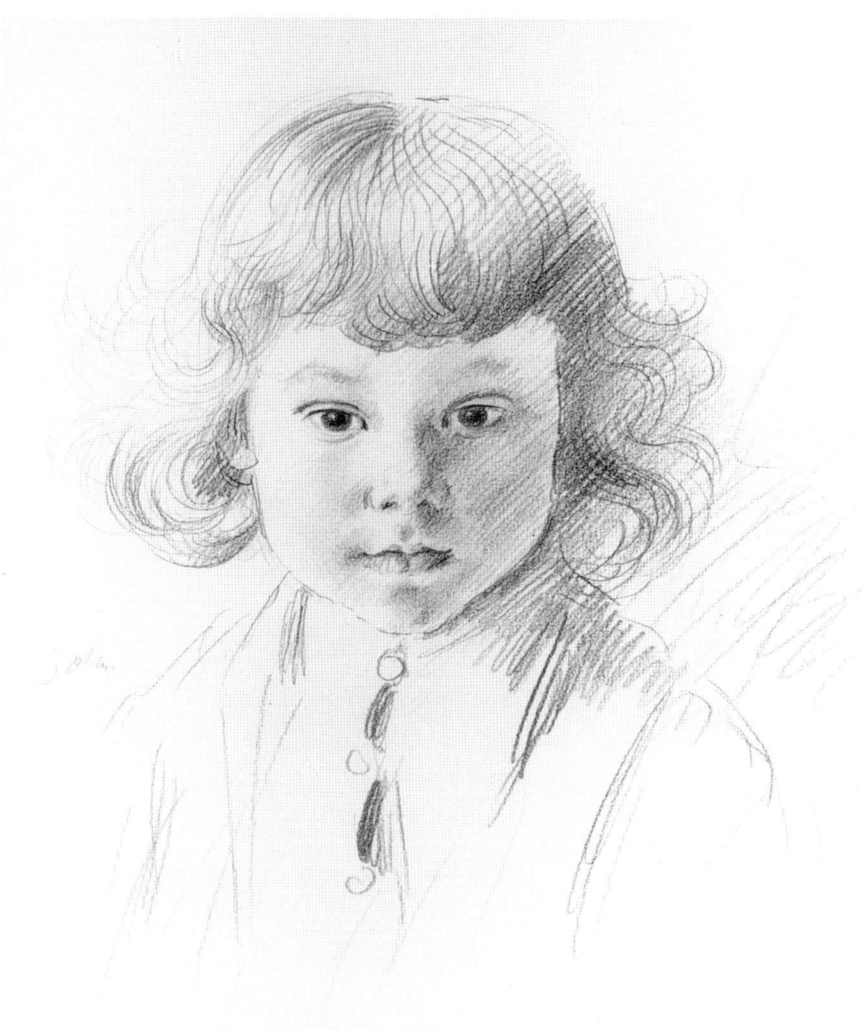

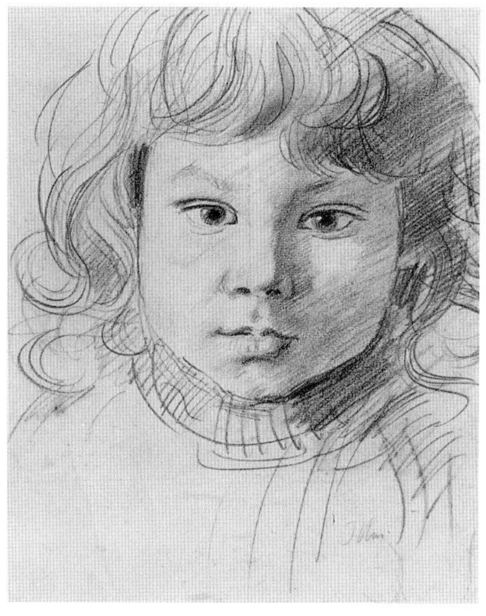

Fig.3 *Head of Caspar John, aged 3*, pencil, whereabouts unknown

23

These drawings of Caspar John (1903-84) were made in Paris after Ida and Dorelia had decamped there in 1905. 'Caspar has just come up from the studio, very hot, remarking "He gave me a penny". I suppose he's been sitting', Ida wrote home in 1906 (R. John, *Caspar John*, London 1987, p.20). Both drawings highlight his almond-shaped eyes, which distinguished him from all his brothers. The cocked hat (Cat.24) was later regarded with amusement by the sitter; he was a founding father of the Fleet Air Arm, and was promoted Admiral in 1957 and First Sea Lord in 1960. By the time he attained Admiral's rank, his bushy eyebrows (a subject of jest at home) and dark eyes had an intimidating effect on strangers. A third drawing (Fig.3, whereabouts unknown) is more closely related to Cat.23.

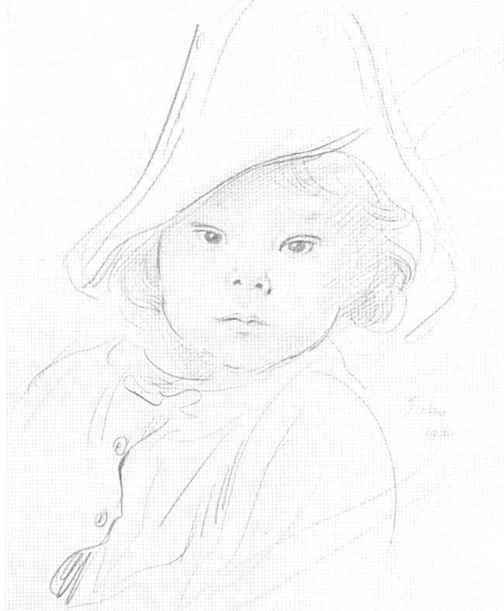

24

23 *Caspar (Head of a child)*
pencil, 25.4×24.7 cm (10×9¾ in)
Signed: *John* (centre, left)
PROV: Purchased from the artist
Collection of the late Morton H. Sands

24 *Head of Caspar John in a cocked hat, aged 3, 1906*
pencil, 27×21.3 cm (10⅝×8⅜ in)
Signed: *John 1906* (centre, right)
LIT: exh. Hull 1970, no.54; exh. London 1974, no.97
PROV: Sir Caspar John; Lady John
Private Collection

Edie McNeill, 1906

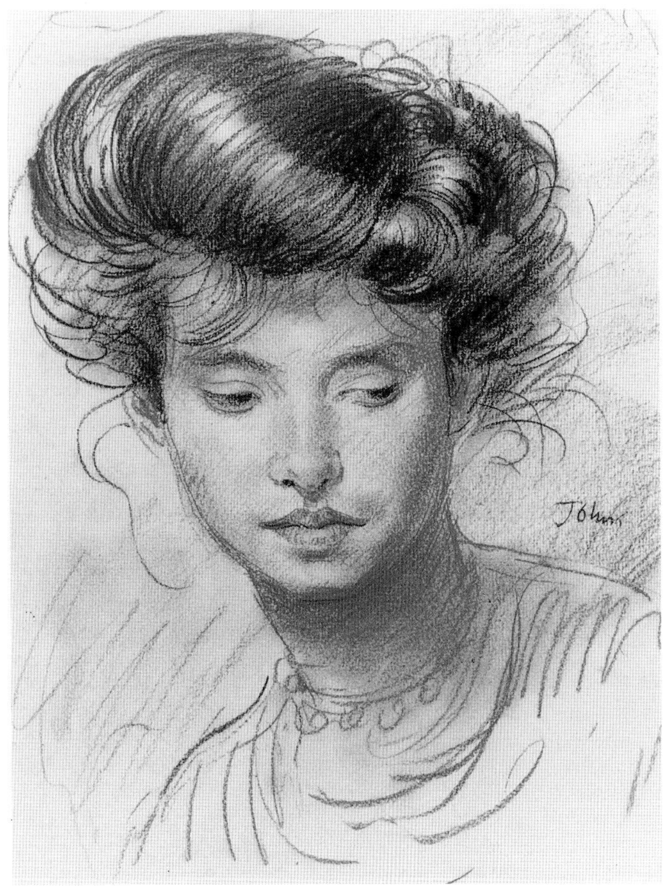

25 (Front cover)

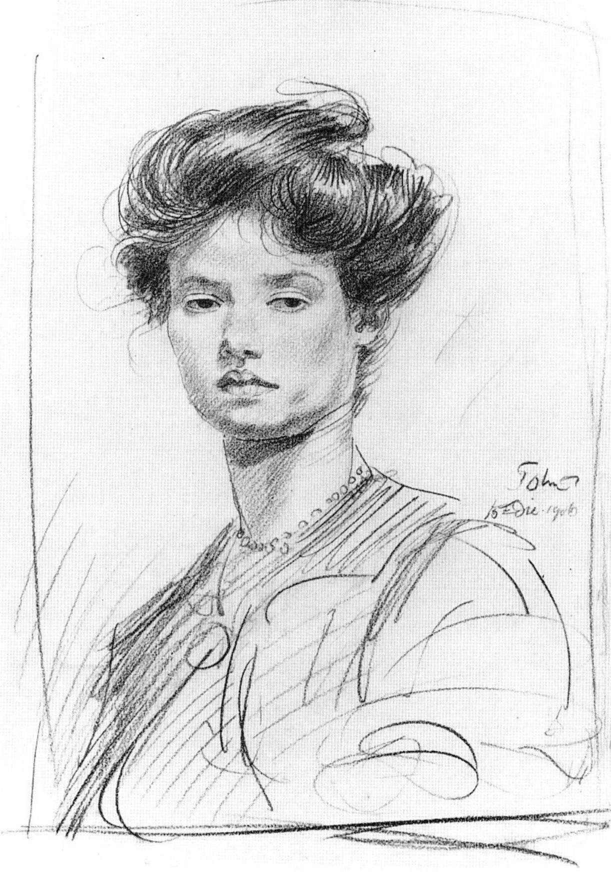

Fig.4 *Head of Edie McNeill*, pencil, private collection, USA

Edie McNeill, Dorelia's sister, came to help with the boys after Ida died in 1907 and later took charge of the kitchen at Alderney Manor while Dorelia went on to have two daughters. Holroyd describes her (1996, pp.366-7): 'Small, with black-brown hair and large brooding eyes, their upper lids curiously straight giving them a strange rectangular shape. Her mouth was rather prominent, curving downwards, and her expression sardonic yet vulnerable – an index of her life to come'. Her niece, Poppet, remembers being taken for drives by her with a pony and a 'sort of platform on wheels which had no sides, so we had the impression of going very fast'. She had a fondness for 'Gin and It', and was nicknamed by the children 'Edie-with-a-hilly-nose', a feature played down here and in its companion (Fig.4, private collection, USA). The latter is dated 10 December 1906. Although in different media, the magnificent head of hair, the necklace, and the paper's dimensions, indicate that these two portraits were drawn in close succession.

25 *Head of a girl (Edie McNeill)*
red and black chalk, 32.5 × 24 cm
($12\frac{7}{8} \times 9\frac{1}{2}$ in)
Signed: *John* (centre, right)
LIT: exh. London 1954, no.94
PROV: Anthony Lousada
Private Collection

Alexandra 'Alick' Schepeler, 1906-7

John's description of Alick Schepeler as being 'of Slavonic origin' is explained by the fact that she had an Irish mother, German father, was born in Russia (in 1882) and raised in Poland. She came to London and worked as a secretary on *The Illustrated London News* where she remained for fifty years. Holroyd's account of their affair is one of the most amusing episodes in his biography (1996, pp.209-15): 'In the extent of her ordinariness lay her single extraordinary quality. She had nothing to hide, but from the presence of this nothing arose a mystery none could solve … her most bewitching quality was her gurgling voice, rich and soupy.' John recalled her 'infinite capacity for laughter … laughter and sometimes tears' (*Autobiography*, p.61).

Like him, she was prone to melancholia, bouts of ennui and loneliness, and the portraits (Cats 26 and 27) give this impression. Are the famous eyes of the Fitzwilliam's portrait (Cat.28) glazed with boredom, or wet with tears of extreme melancholia? John liked to fancy her as a creature from another world: in the *Study for an Undine* (Cat.29) she appears to have already changed into the water sprite she becomes in *Study of an Undine* (Cat.30). At least eighteen portrait heads of Alick Schepeler are known, and there are probably others. Even John recalled that he made 'many drawings' of her, although the best painting, titled *La Seraphita* was accidentally destroyed in a fire.

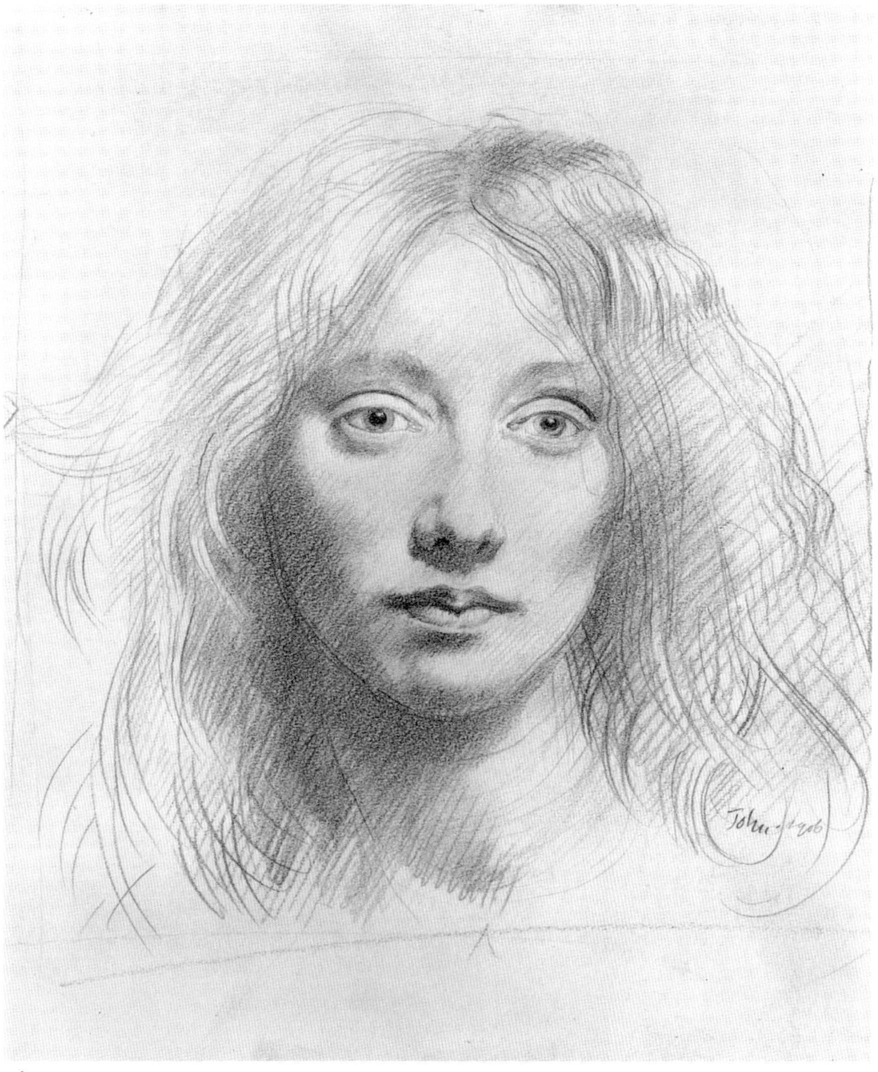

26

26   *Portrait of Alexandra (Alick) Schepeler, 1906*
pencil, 35.6 × 29.1 cm (14 × 11¼ in)
Signed: *John 1906* (lower right)
LIT: exh. London 1940, no.92; London 1954, no.76; Longstreet 1967, p.5; exh.London 1974, no.60; Easton and Holroyd 1974, no.37; exh. Cambridge 1978, no.44
PROV: Chenil Gallery; Dr Louis C. G. Clarke; by whom bequeathed, 1961
Lent by the Syndics of the Fitzwilliam Museum, Cambridge (PD.154-1961)

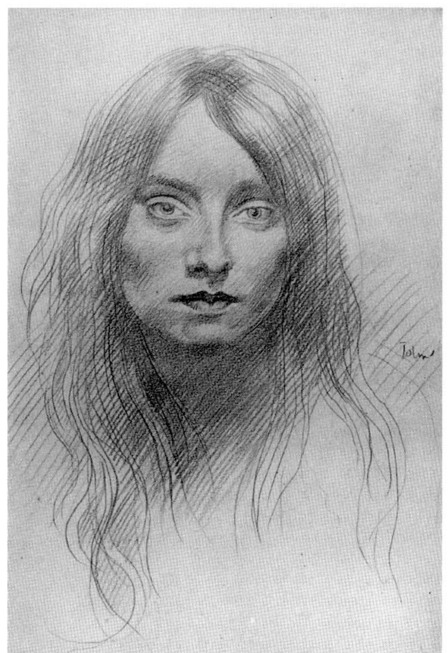

27

27   *Head of Alexandra (Alick) Schepeler*
pencil, 28.2 × 18.2 cm (11¼ × 7⅛ in)
Signed: *John* (centre, right)
LIT: exh. London 1965, no.51; Cambridge 1978, no.45
PROV: Mrs Clifton; Thos Agnew & Sons; Peter Harris; by whom bequeathed, 1976
Lent by the Syndics of the Fitzwilliam Museum, Cambridge (PD.24-1976)

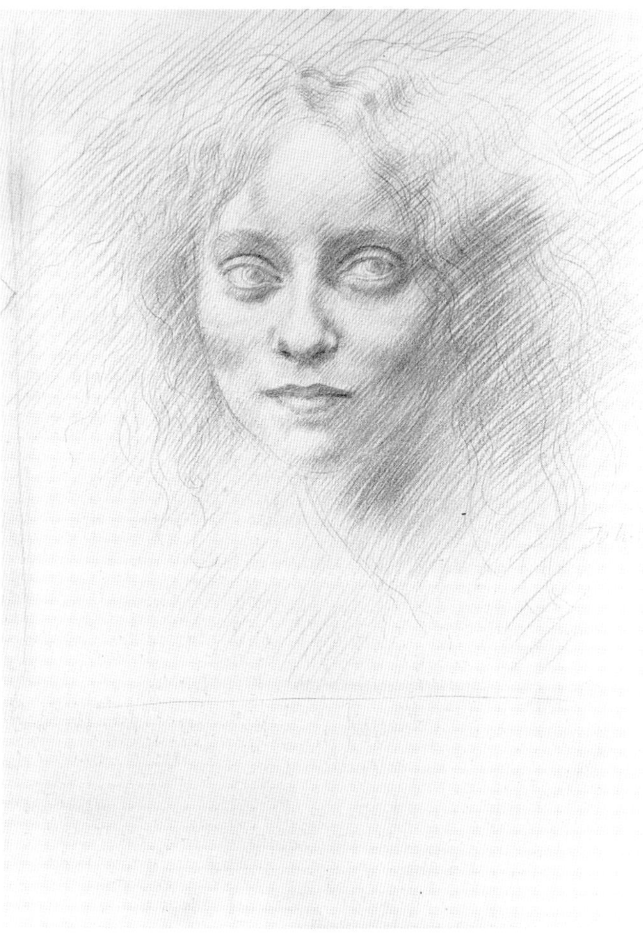

28

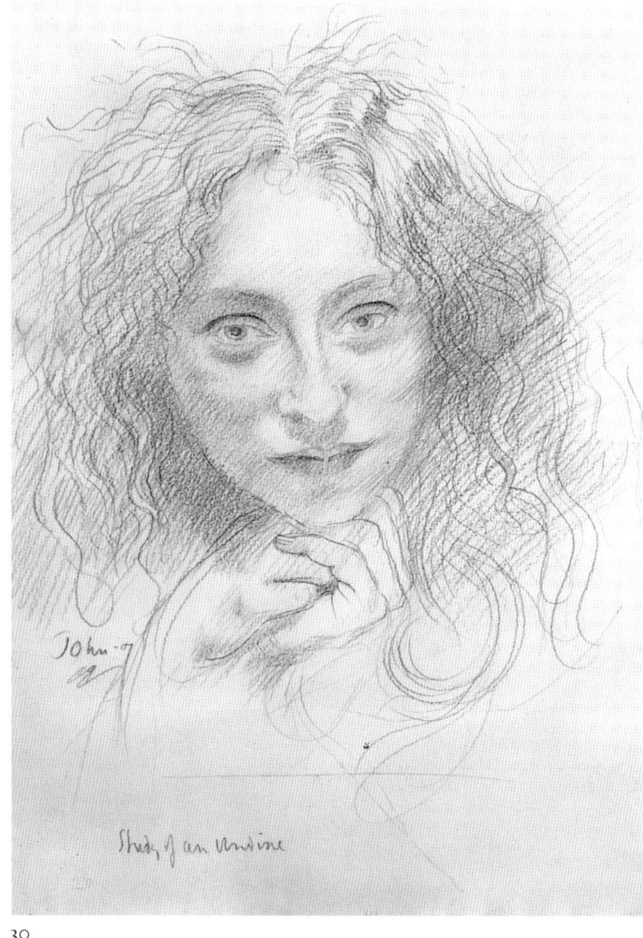

30

28 *Study of a woman's head*
pencil, 35.5×25.3 cm (14×10 in)
Signed: *John* (lower right)
LIT: exh. London 1974, no.62;
Cambridge 1978, no.42
PROV: Sir Herbert Thompson Bt; by
whom given, 1920
Lent by the Syndics of the Fitzwilliam
Museum, Cambridge (No. 1024)

29 *Study for an Undine (Alick Schepeler),*
1906
pencil, 35.7×25.7 cm (14×10$\frac{1}{8}$ in)
Signed: *John 1906* (bottom right)
LIT: exh. London 1954, no.85; Longstreet
1967, p.34; exh. London 1974, no.61
PROV: Charles L. Rutherston; by whom
presented, 1925
Lent by Manchester City Art Galleries
(1925.367)

30 *Study of an Undine, 1907*
pencil, 37.3×25.5 cm (14$\frac{3}{4}$×10 in)
Signed: *John – 07* (lower left)
Inscribed (by the artist): *Study of an*
Undine (bottom, centre/left)
LIT: exh. Cambridge 1978, no.43
PROV: Dr Louis C.G. Clarke; by whom
bequeathed, 1961
Lent by the Syndics of the Fitzwilliam
Museum, Cambridge (PD.155-1961)

31 *Head of Alick Schepeler*
pencil on discoloured greyish white
paper, 22.9×21.6 cm (9×8$\frac{1}{2}$ in)
Signed: *John* (bottom right)
PROV: T. W. Bacon
Private Collection

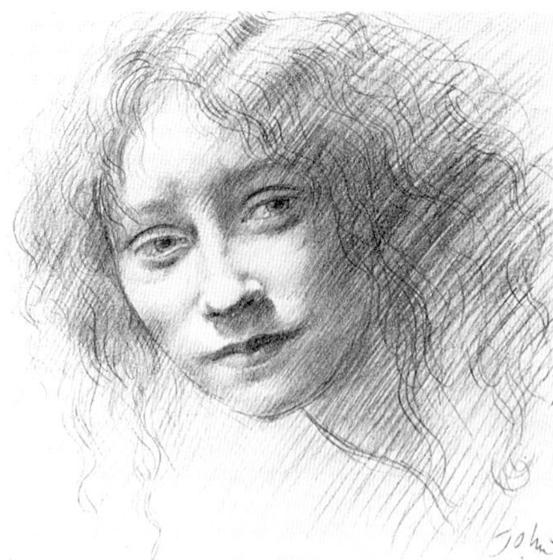

31 (Colour plate 5)

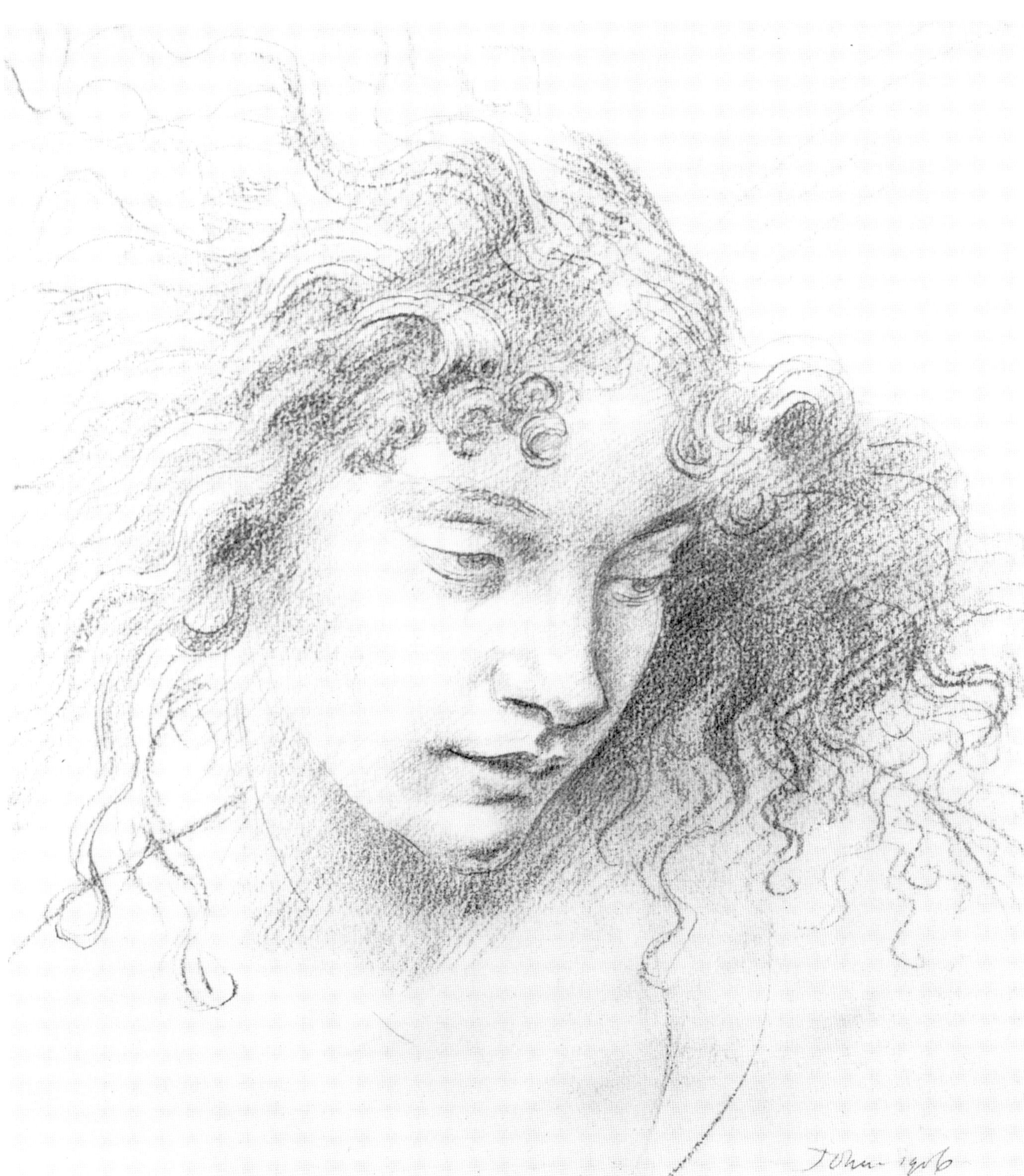

29

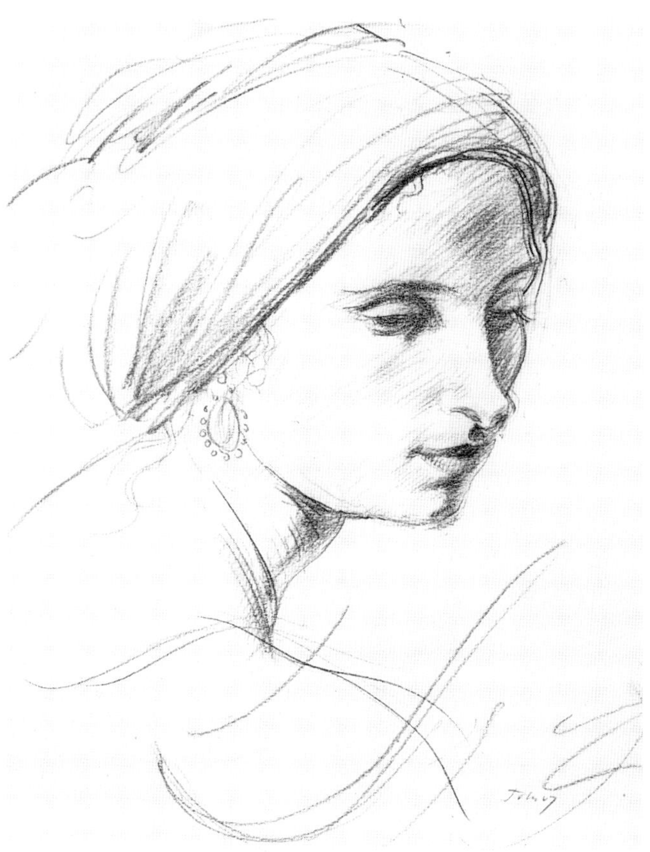

32 (Colour plate 4)

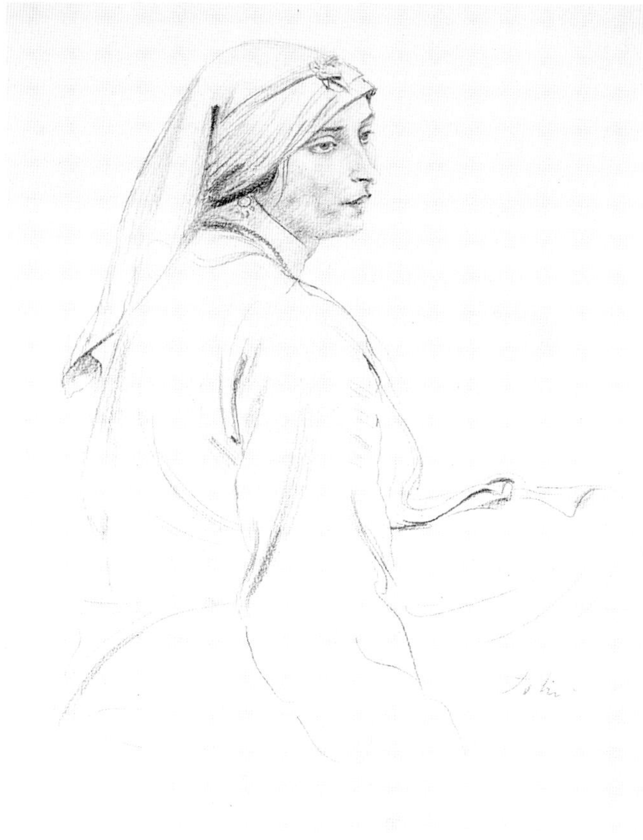

33

These portraits depict the sitter in similar costume and in the same three-quarter turned stance. They are characterised by longer, flowing lines and are freer in execution than the finely worked full-face portrait heads of 1903-4 and 1909.

32 *Dorelia with earrings, 1907*
red chalk, 31.7 × 24.1 cm ($12\frac{1}{2} \times 9\frac{1}{2}$ in)
Signed: *John* 07 (bottom right)
PROV: Alfred Jowett; Anthony D'Offay Gallery
Private Collection

33 *Bust of Dorelia with earrings*
pencil, 36.8 × 29.4 cm ($14\frac{1}{2} \times 11\frac{5}{8}$ in)
Signed: *John* (lower right)
Spink & Son Ltd

Fishergirl of Equihen, 1907

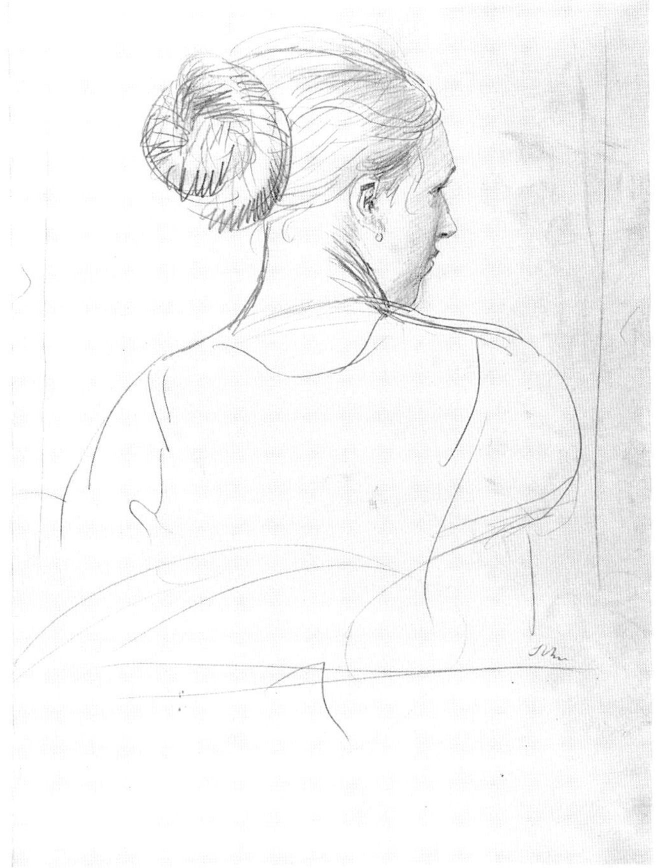

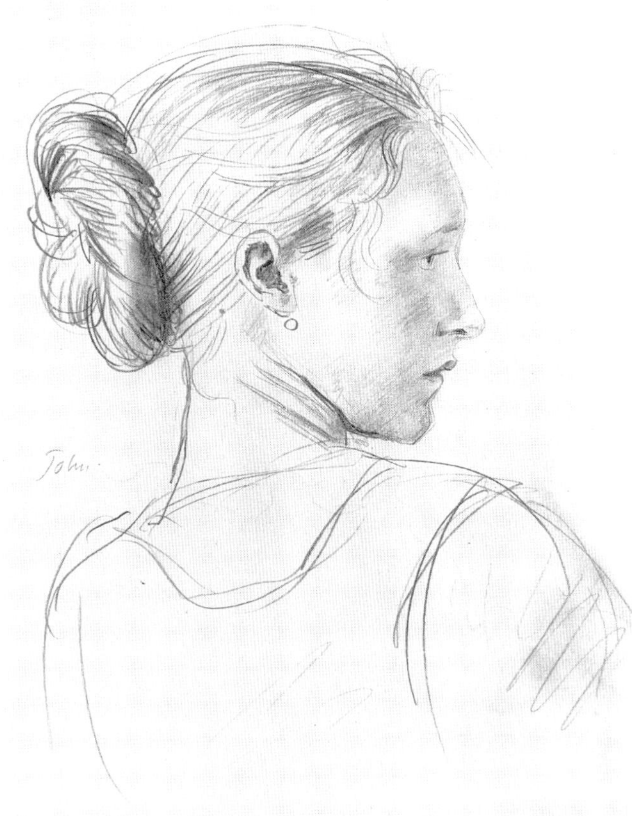

34

Fig.5 *Fishergirl of Equihen, profile,* pencil, private collection

Four single-figure drawings of this French fishergirl were reproduced in Lillian Browse's *Augustus John. Drawings* (1942). At least eleven are known, of which six are assembled here (Cats 34-9 and Fig.5, private collection). This series appears to have been executed in rapid succession as the artist circled his model. John also made studies of other Equihen fishergirls and several group compositions, incorporating figures derived from the studies (Cat.41). Recalling the market days of his childhood in Pembrokeshire, he described 'the women of Langum, in their distinctive costume, carrying creels of the famous oysters on their backs' (*Autobiography*, p.22). When, in the summer of 1907, he came across a group of fishergirls working on the Normandy coast at Equihen, he was again struck by their 'distinctive costumes' and later wrote:

'With the rise of a new bourgeoisie, flourishing on the principles of self-help, child-torture and mass-enslavement, all manifestations of the folk-spirit were frowned upon as vulgar and un-Christian: the old songs and dances were gradually forgotten, and the hereditary costumes folded and put away, to be replaced by the shoddy products of the factory: and now that the country crafts have gone too, there is not much joy left in the land. The *genius loci* has become a disreputable character, interesting only to the policeman' (*Autobiography*, p.326).

34 *Fishergirl of Equihen, from behind*
pencil, 35×25.3 cm (13¾×10 in)
Signed: *John* (bottom right)
LIT: exh. Cardiff 1978, no.64
PROV: Miss R. Spooner; by whom given in memory of Catherine Dodgson, 1954
Lent by the Trustees of the British Museum (1954-6-10-15)
[Exhibited in Cardiff and Conwy only]

OVERLEAF
35 *Fishergirl of Equihen, with hands on hips*
pencil, 27.3×24.1 cm (10¾×9½ in)
Signed: *John* (bottom right)
LIT: exh. London 1940, no.35; London 1954, no.243; Cardiff 1978, no.62
PROV: Mrs Mona Hamilton Watkins; Charles Hill; Roland, Browse & Delbanco; from whom purchased, 1948
Lent by the City Museum and Art Gallery, Birmingham (P.11'48)

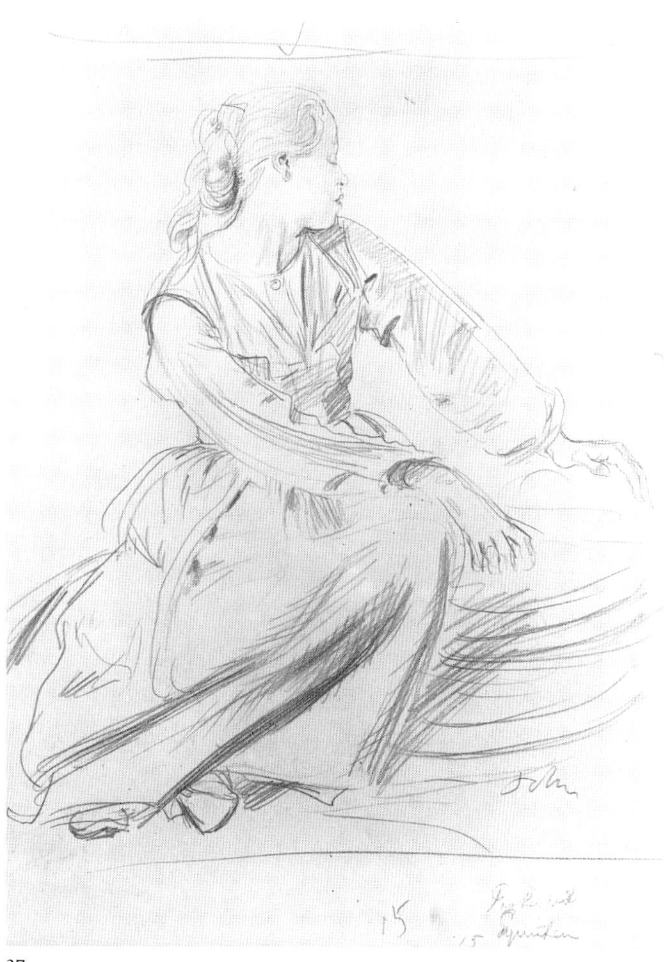

37

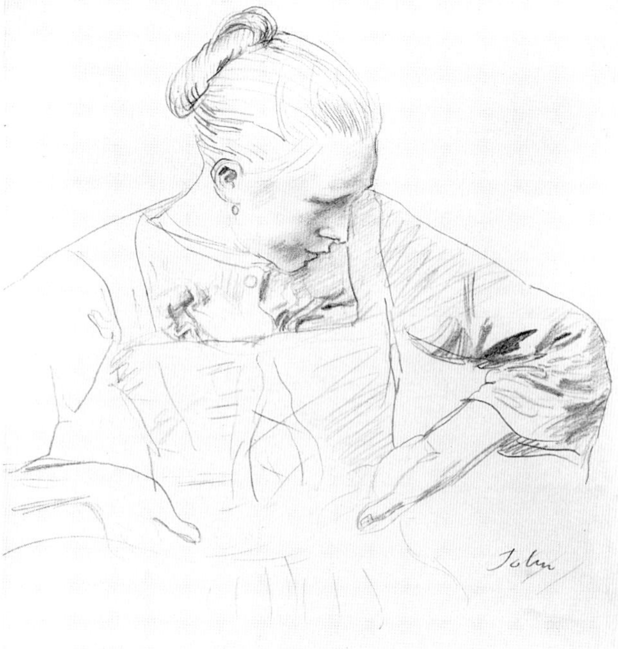

36

36 *Fishergirl of Equihen, full length with
hands on hips*
pencil, 35.5×22.8 cm (14×9 in)
Signed: *John* (bottom right)
LIT: Browse 1942, no.24
Private Collection

37 *Fishergirl of Equihen, full length,
turning away*
pencil, 27.3×24.1 cm (11¾×9¾ in)
Signed: *John* (bottom right)
Inscribed (by the artist):
Fishergirl / Equihen (bottom right)
LIT: Browse 1942, no.26; exh. London
1948, no.63; London 1954, no.246; exh.
Cardiff 1978, no.63
PROV: Harry Collison; by whom
presented
Lent by the Warden and Scholars of
Winchester College

35

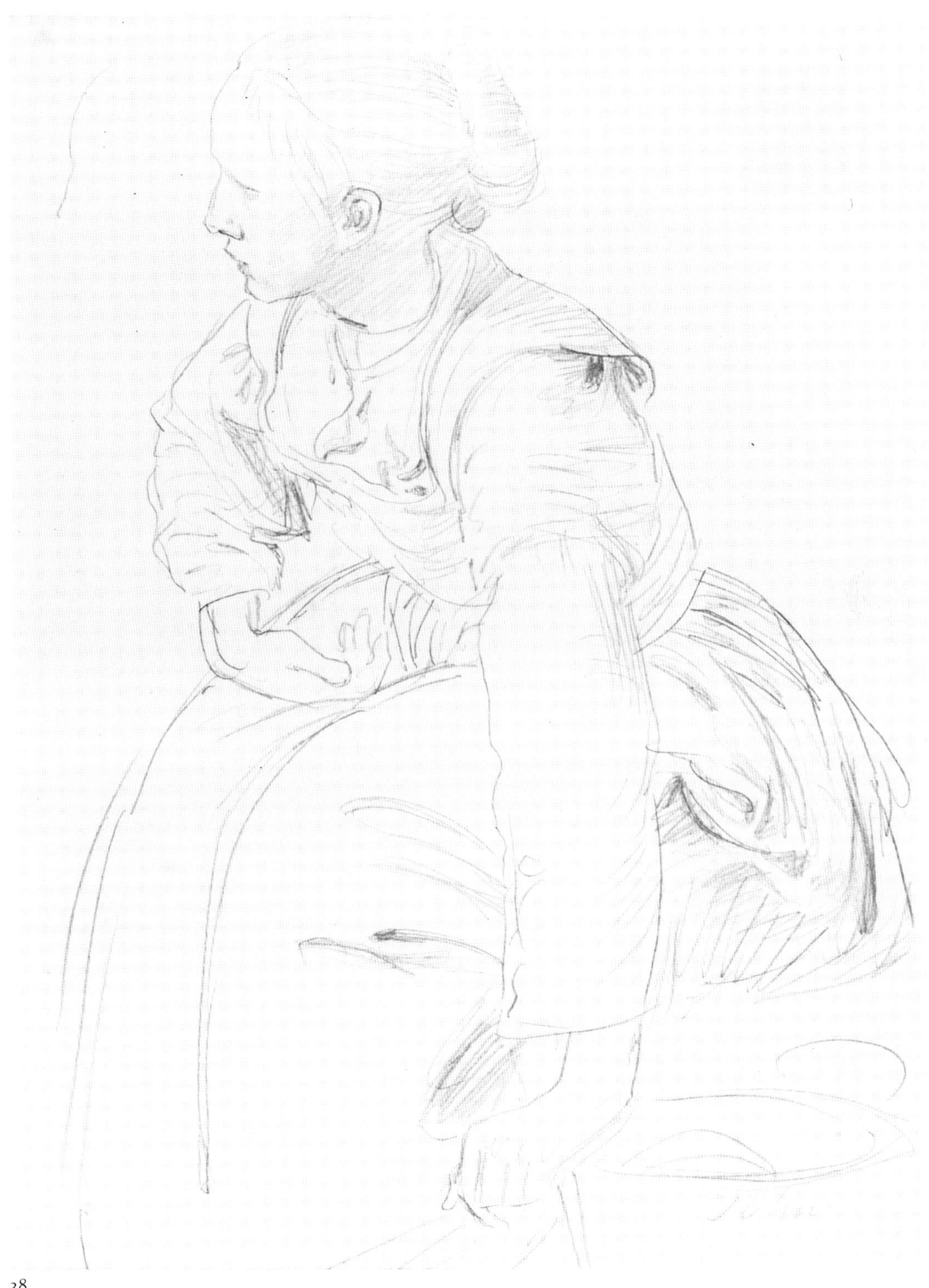

38

38 *Fishergirl of Equihen, to left*
pencil, 24×17.5 cm (9½×6⅞ in)
Signed: *John* (bottom right)
LIT: Browse 1942, no.27
PROV: Lady Cottesloe
Private Collection

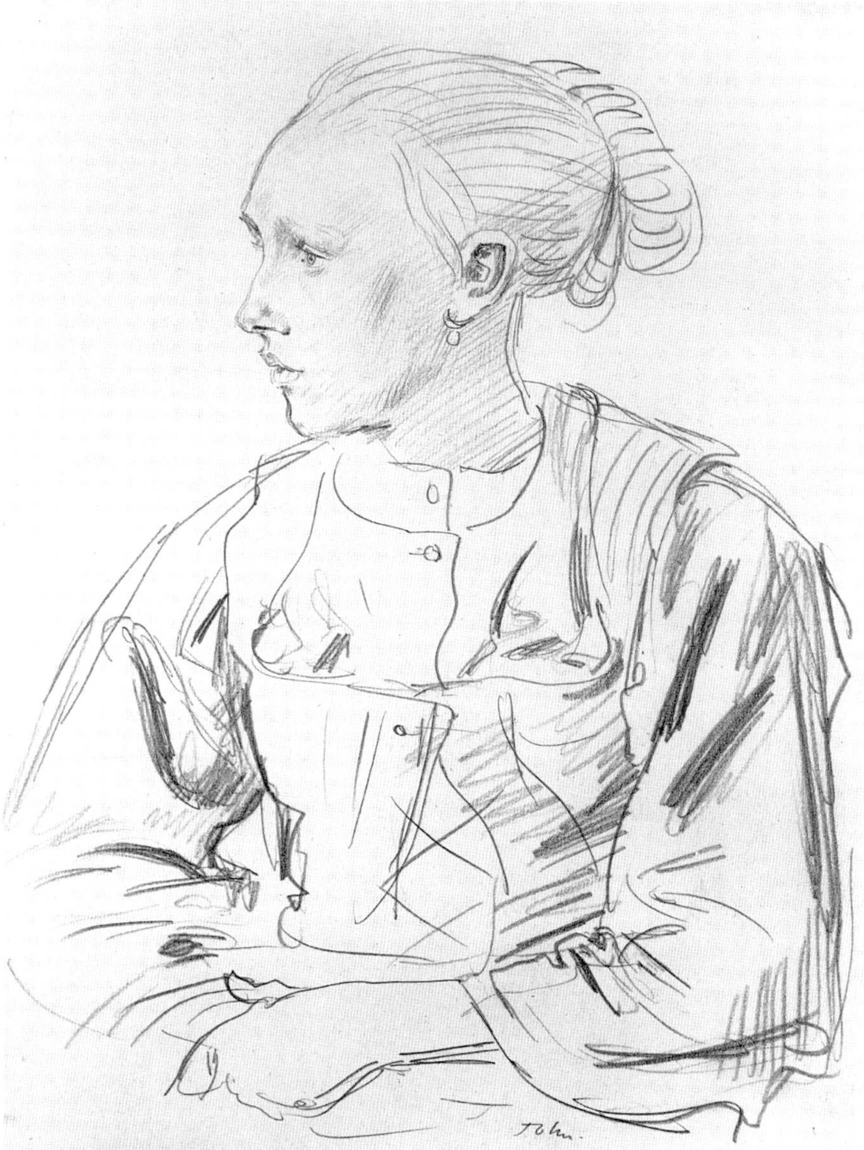

39

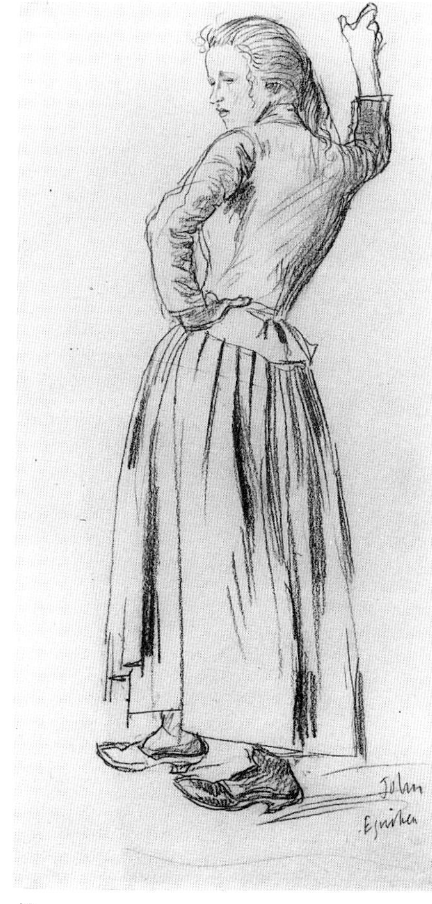

40

39 *Fishergirl of Equihen, in profile to left*
pencil on grey-brown paper,
29.4×22 cm (11½×8⅝ in)
Signed: *John* (bottom centre/right)
LIT: exh. Cardiff 1978, no.65
PROV: Mrs W. R. F. Weldon; by whom
bequeathed, 1937
Lent by the Visitors of the Ashmolean
Museum, Oxford (Acc.no.1937.26)

40 *Fishergirl of Equihen*
(Study of a standing fishergirl)
black chalk, 35.5×18.4 cm (14×7¼ in)
Signed: *John/Equihen* (bottom right)
LIT: exh. London 1974, no.125
PROV: Leicester Galleries; from whom
purchased, 1939
Lent by Bristol Museums and Art Gallery
(MD 3421)

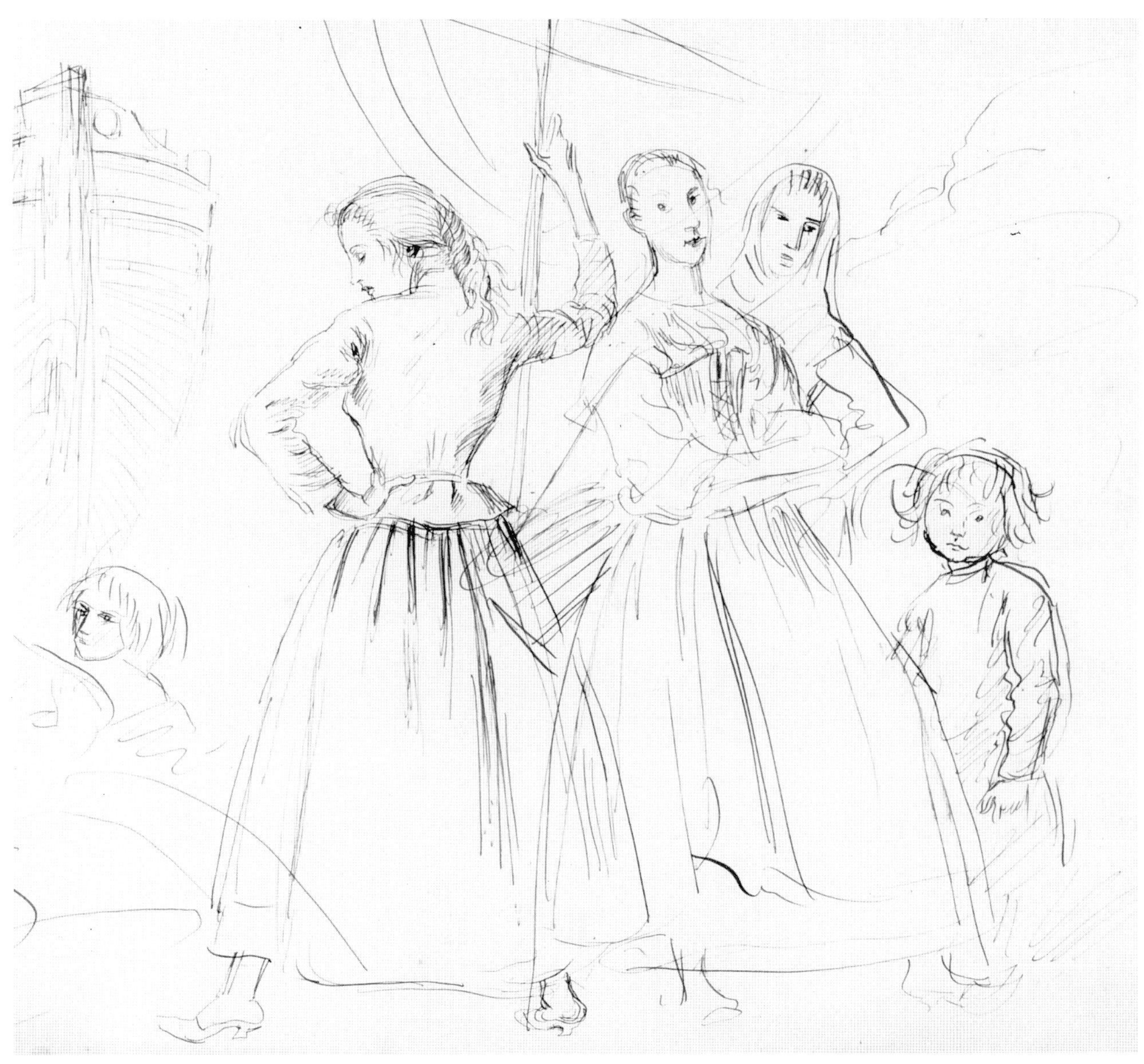

41

41 *Fishergirls on the beach at Equihen*
ink, 34.3×36.8 cm (13½×14½ in)
LIT: exh. London 1954, no.248; London
1974, no.124
Lent by Sir Brinsley Ford CBE Hon.FRA
FSA

William Butler Yeats, 1907

In 1907 John visited Coole Park, County Galway, the residence of Lady Gregory, to execute an oil portrait (Manchester City Art Gallery) and an etching of the famous Irish poet W. B. Yeats (1865-1939). The etching was commissioned as a frontispiece for a new edition of the poet's *Collected Works*. Faced with the complaints of Yeats that John's likeness made him seem 'a sheer tinker, drunken, unpleasant and disreputable, but full of wisdom' and the more violent objection of Lady Gregory ('if they are not like Yeats … they and the plate shall go into the fire'), the artist produced 'numberless' studies and a total of five plates, the last in four states. Although Yeats conceded that the final result was a 'beautiful etching', he found it 'useless for my special purpose' and it was not used for the frontispiece (Holroyd 1996, pp.243-4). Despite this disagreement, John remained on the best of terms with Yeats and painted another oil portrait of him in 1930 (Glasgow Art Gallery and Museum).

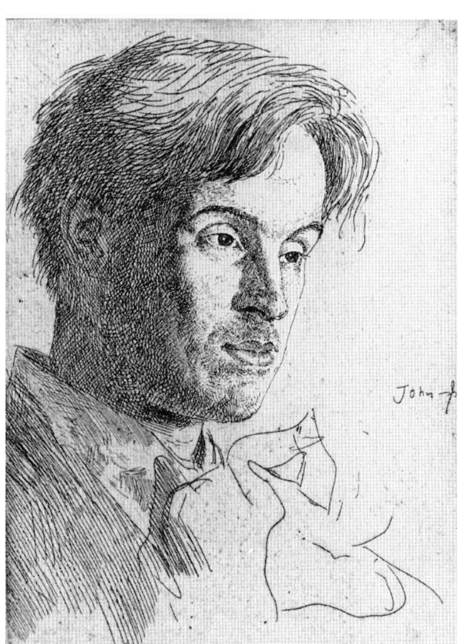

42

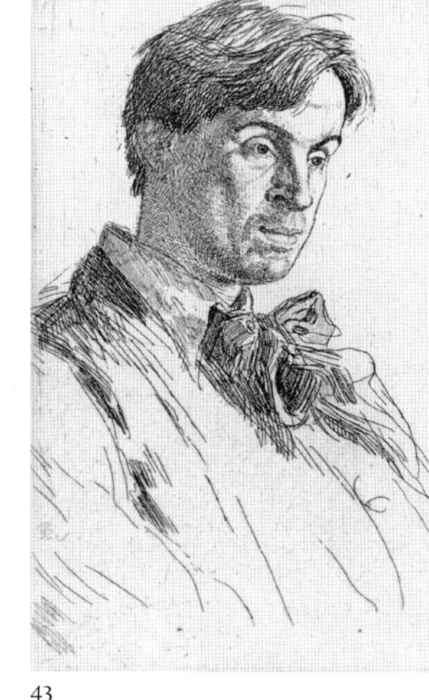

43

42 *William Butler Yeats: first plate*
etching, 17.8×12.5 cm (7×5 in)
Incised: *John f.* (lower right, in the plate)
Signed: *John* (in pencil, bottom right, below plate)
LIT: Campbell Dodgson 1920, no.24; exh. Cardiff 1988, no.14
PROV: Presented by the artist, 1920
National Museum and Gallery, Cardiff
(NMW A3481)

43 *William Butler Yeats: fourth plate*
etching, 17.6×12.8 cm (6⅞×5 in)
Incised: *John* (upper right, in the plate)
Signed: *John* (in pencil, bottom right, below plate)
LIT: Campbell Dodgson 1920, no.27
PROV: Presented by the artist, 1920
National Museum and Gallery, Cardiff
(NMW A3665)

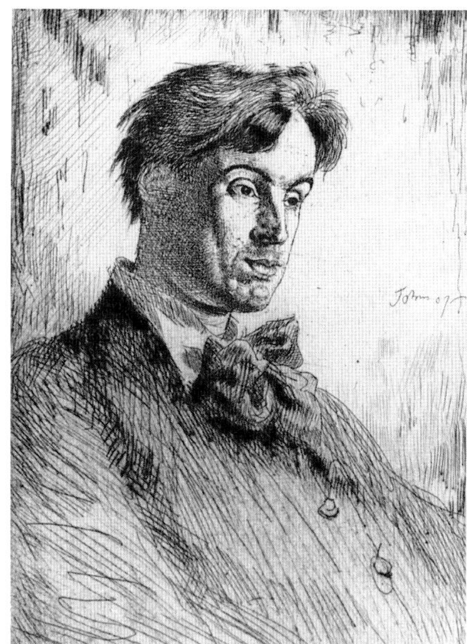

44

44 *William Butler Yeats: fifth plate*
etching, 17.6×12.8 cm (6⅞×5 in)
Incised: *John 07* (centre, right, in the plate)
Signed: *John* (in pencil, bottom right, below plate)
LIT: Campbell Dodgson 1920, no.28, state IV
PROV: Presented by the artist, 1920
National Museum and Gallery, Cardiff
(NMW A3666)

Dorelia, full length, arm over head, 1908

This trio of drawings portrays Dorelia subtly changing pose by slight shifts of the feet, arms and head. Two other versions in this series are known, one of which depicts her from behind and is dated 1908 (Browse 1942, no.43). John incorporated this pose in the large oil painting *The way down to the sea* (private collection), first exhibited in 1909, in which Dorelia is reunited with the posthumous figure of Ida (see Cats 5-8).

45 *Dorelia standing with right arm above her head*
pencil, 46×25.4 cm (18⅛×10 in)
Signed: *John* (bottom right)
LIT: *Drawings from the Alfred A. De Pass collection belonging to the Royal Institution of Truro, Cornwall*, Arts Council of Great Britain, London 1957, no.52
PROV: Alfred De Pass; by whom presented, 1924
Lent by the Royal Institution of Cornwall, Royal Cornwall Museum, Truro (1924.110)

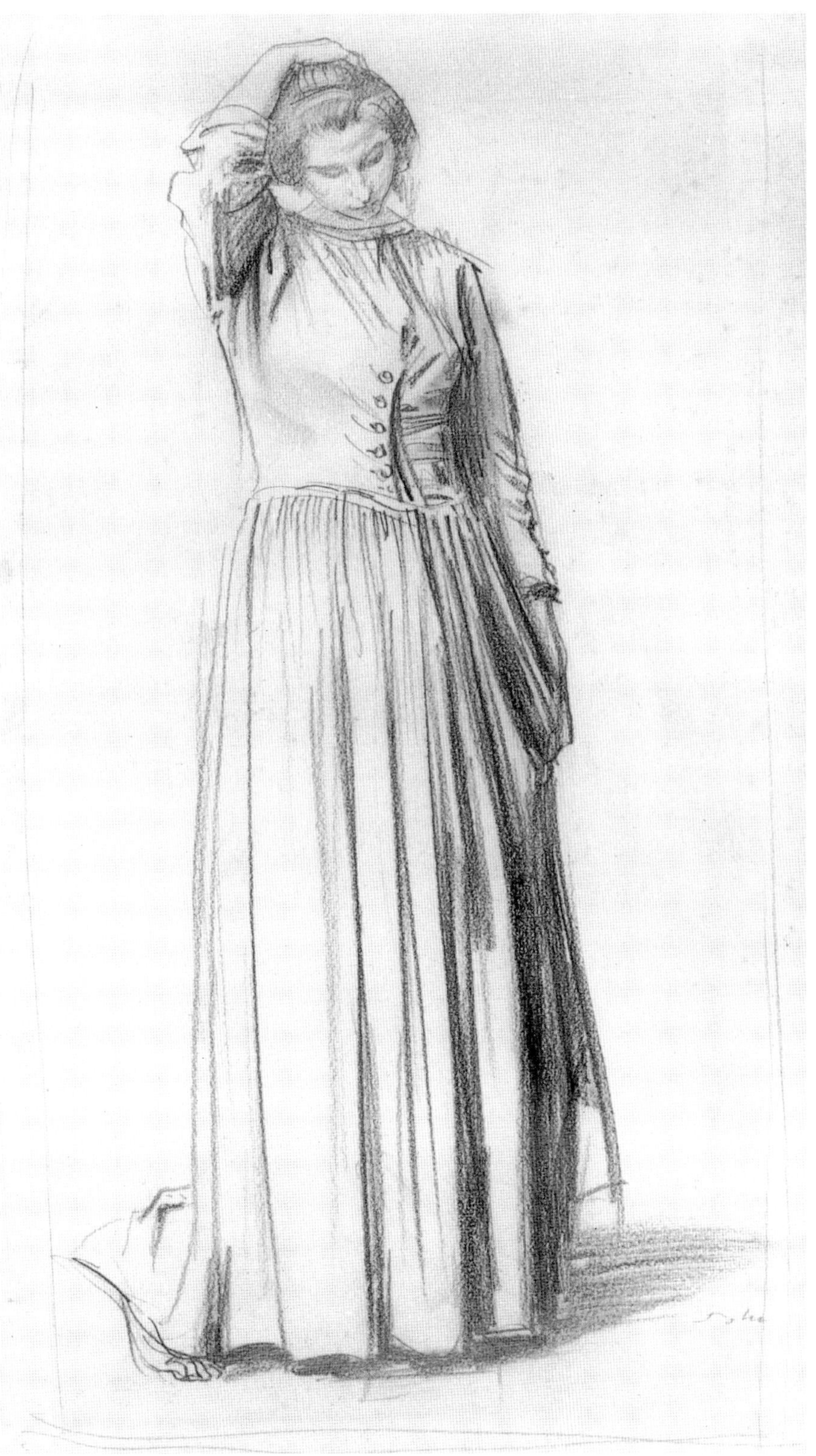

45

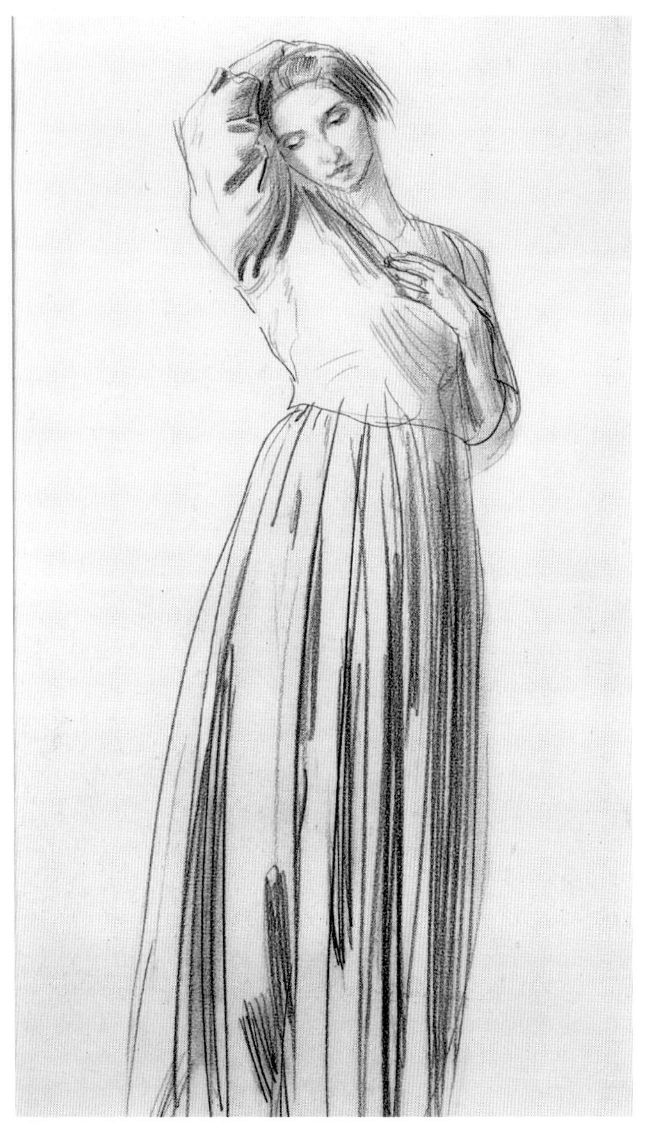

46

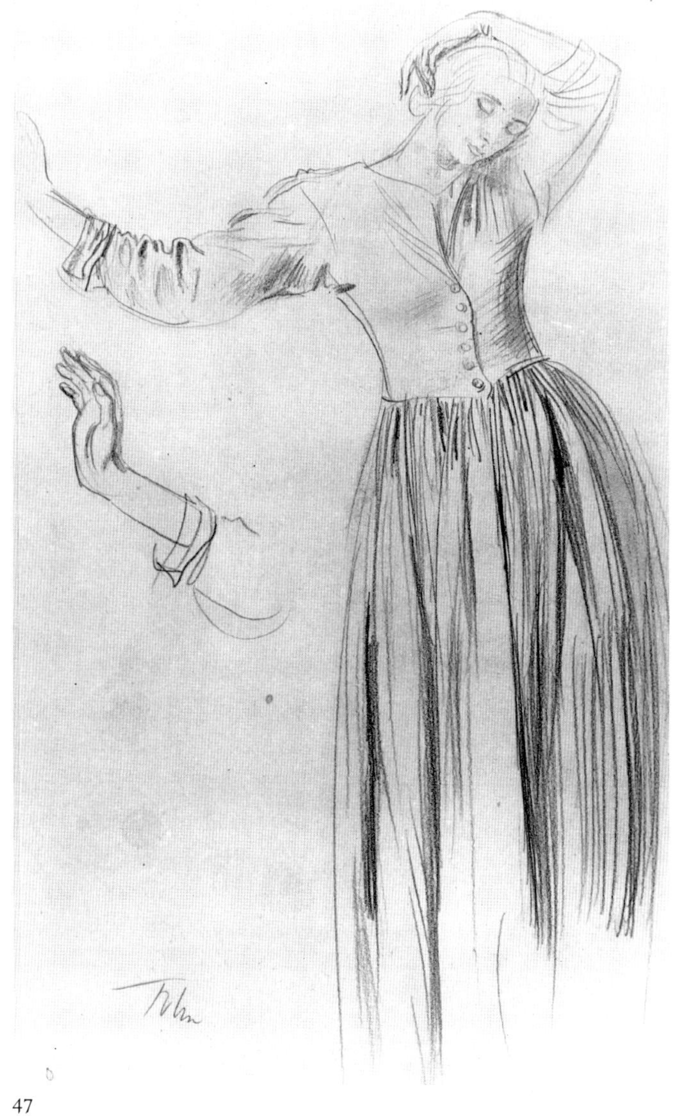

47

46 *Dorelia standing with right arm above her head*
pencil, 37.5×21.3 cm (14¾×8⅜ in)
PROV: Thos Agnew & Sons
Private Collection

47 *Dorelia standing with left arm above her head*
pencil, 44.5×26.8 cm (17½×10½ in)
Signed: *John* (bottom left)
LIT: Browse 1942, no.17
PROV: Charles L. Rutherston; by whom presented, 1925
Lent by Manchester City Art Galleries (1925.376)

Dorelia in a long dress (stepping forward) *c.*1908-9

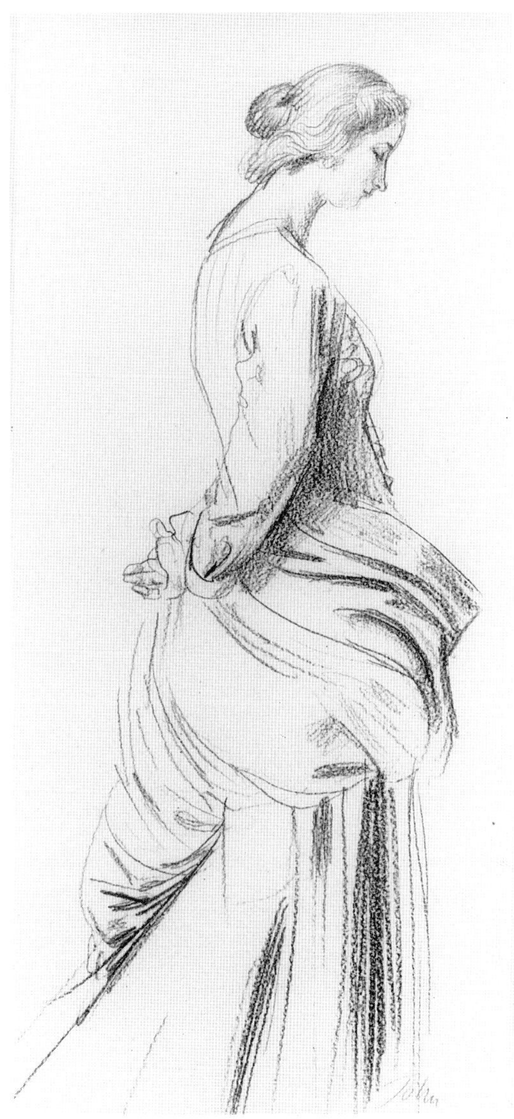

48

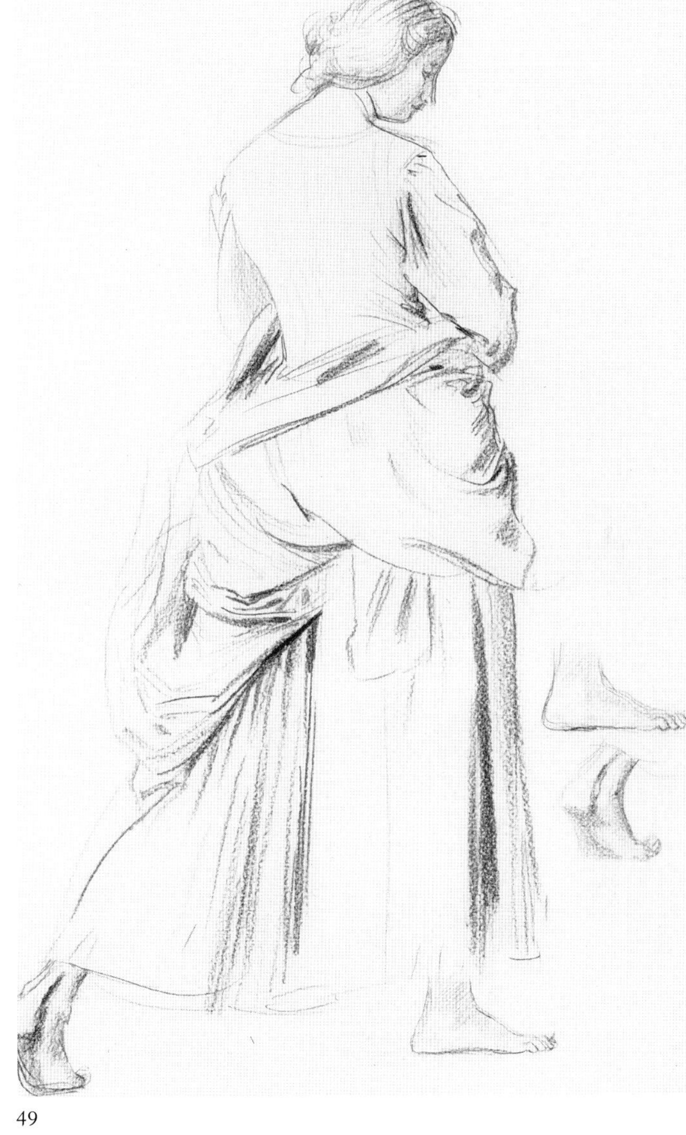

49

A pair of drawings made consecutively, Dorelia having taken a step forward for the second pose. The pose of the figure in Cat.49 reappears, with changed arm positions, in John's oil *Family group* of 1908-9 (Municipal Gallery of Modern Art, Dublin; exh. Cardiff 1978, pl. facing no.82).

48 *Dorelia in a long dress*
pencil, 46.8×16.5 cm (14½×6½ in)
Signed: *John* (bottom right)
LIT: exh. London 1940, no.66; London 1948, no.74; London 1954, no.112
PROV: Purchased from the artist
Collection of the late Morton H. Sands

49 *Dorelia in a long dress, seen from behind*
pencil, 40×24.8 cm (15¾×9¾ in)
PROV: Dr William Messer, sold Sotheby's 21 November 1962, lot 148; Thos Agnew & Sons; from whom purchased, 1966
Private Collection

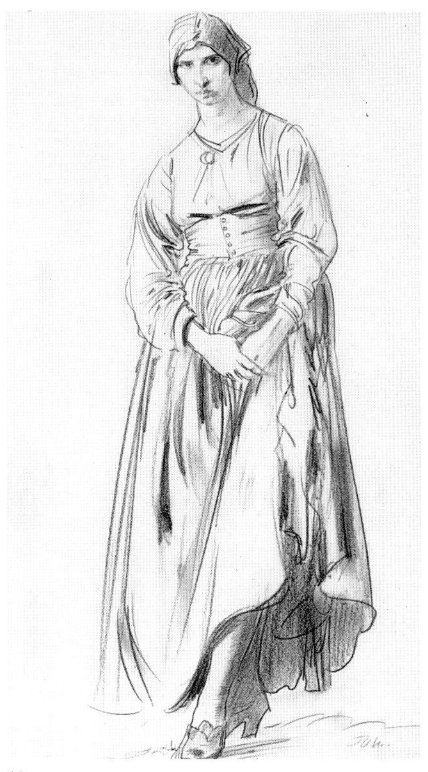

50

Although Dorelia appears to be holding
up her skirt as she steps forward, she
stands with her weight resting on the
foot behind. In Cat.51, the artist has
moved his viewpoint closer and slightly
to the right. The costume and attitude of
the head and torso are analogous to
John's large oil portrait of Dorelia seated
titled *The smiling woman* (Tate Gallery),
first exhibited in 1909.

50 *Dorelia holding up her skirt*
pencil, 49×28.5 cm (19$\frac{1}{4}$×11$\frac{1}{4}$ in)
Signed: *John* (bottom right)
PROV: Arthur Tooth & Sons; Helen Hope
Montgomery and Edgar Scott; sold
Christie's 21 March 1996, lot 63
Private Collection

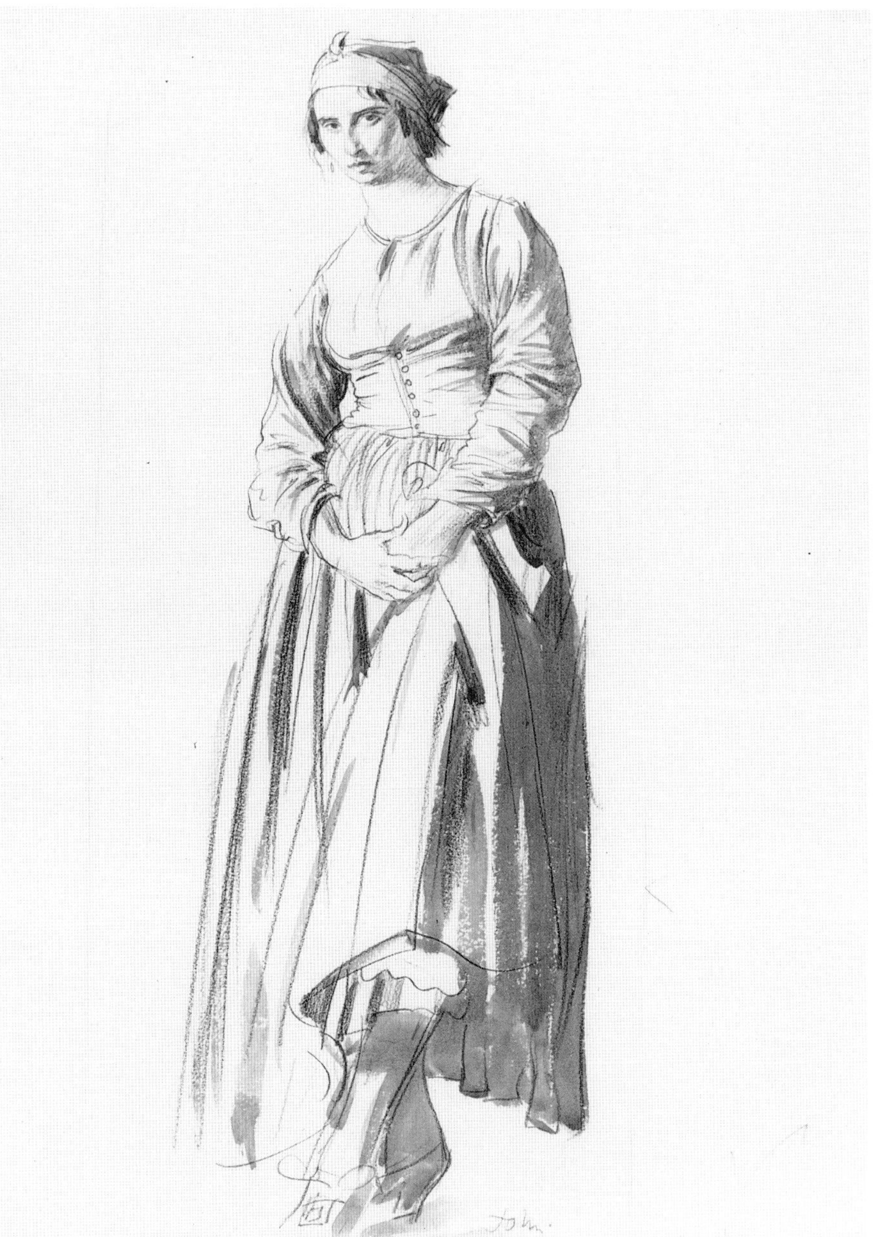

51

51 *Dorelia holding up her skirt*
charcoal and wash, 45.5×27 cm
(18×10$\frac{3}{4}$ in)
Signed: *John* (bottom right)
LIT: Browse 1942, no.33; Rothenstein
1944, p.6; exh. London 1948, no.76
PROV: Lord Henry Cavendish-Bentinck,
Lady Henry Cavendish-Bentinck; by
whom bequeathed, 1940
Lent by the Trustees of the Tate Gallery
(5158)

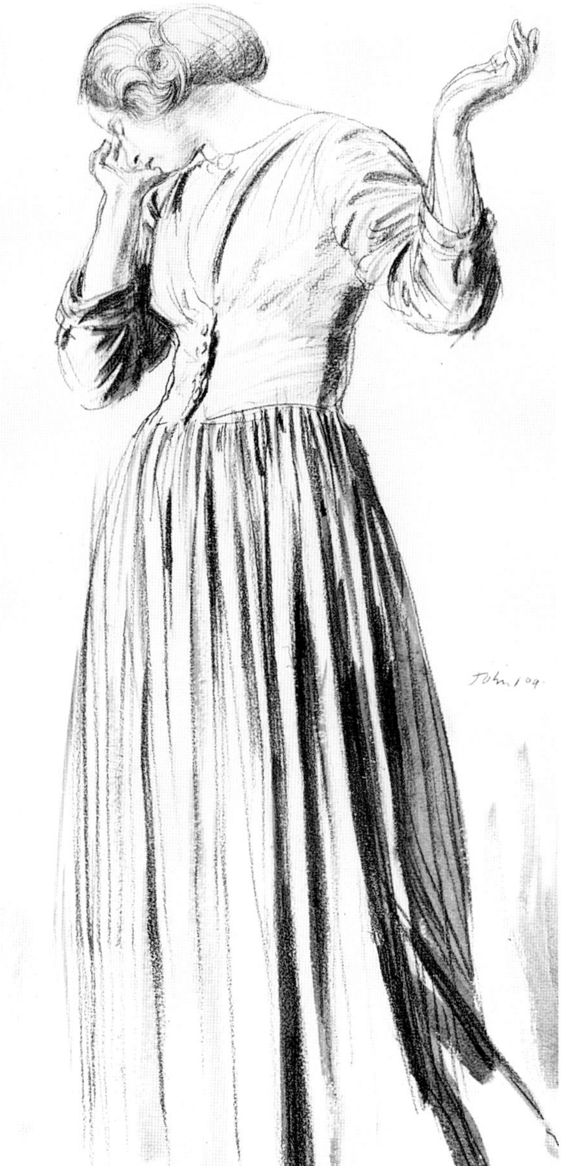

52 (Back cover)

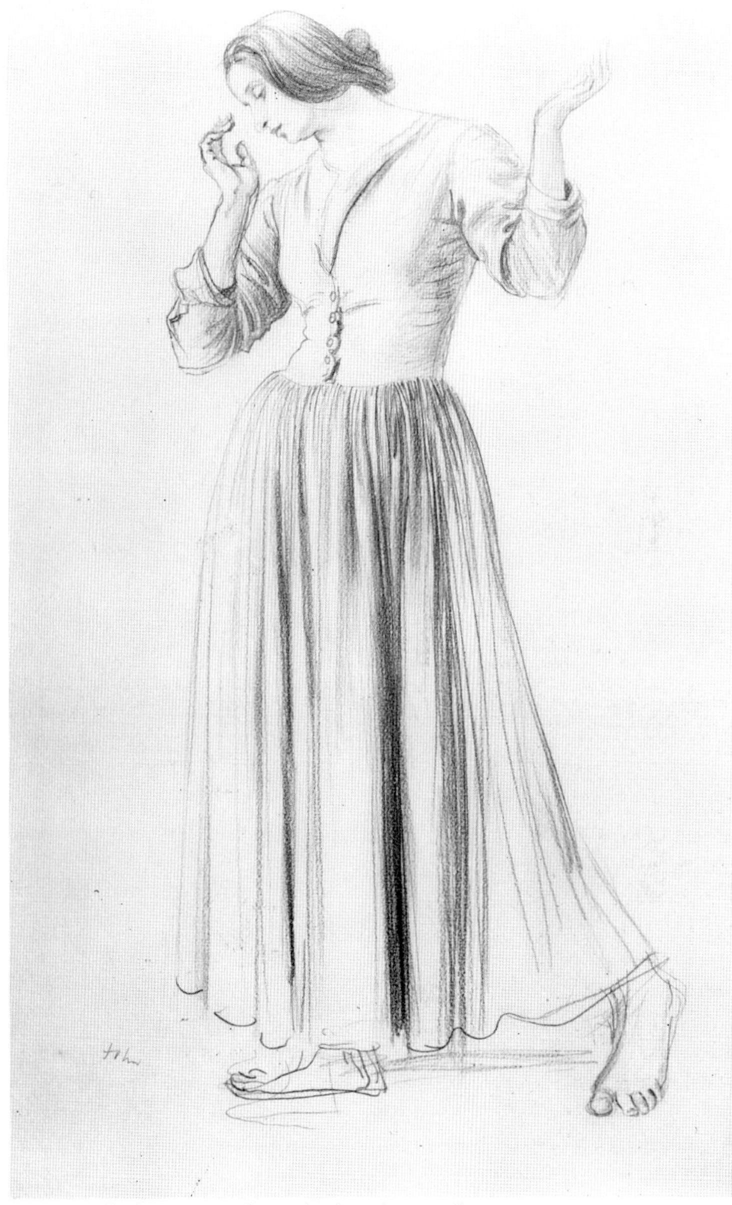

Fig.6 *Dorelia, her arms raised*, pencil, whereabouts unknown

A closely related pencil drawing (Fig.6,
whereabouts unknown) depicts Dorelia
in an identical pose, but with her feet
visible and her right hand held slightly
away from the face. John utilised this
figure in the oil painting *Forza e amore*
(since destroyed), first exhibited in 1911
and intended as part of the decorations
for the entrance hall of Sir Hugh Lane's
house in Chelsea (see exh. Cardiff 1978,
no.111).

52 *Dorelia, her arms raised, 1909*
pencil and wash, 46.3×21.6 cm
($18\frac{1}{4}$×$8\frac{1}{2}$ in)
Signed: *John /09* (centre right)
PROV: Lady Ottoline Morrell; Lady
Henry Cavendish-Bentinck; sold
Sotheby's 28 March 1962, lot 66; Lady
Dodds; Mrs Thelma Cazalet-Keir CBE
Private Collection

Dorelia, portrait heads, 1909

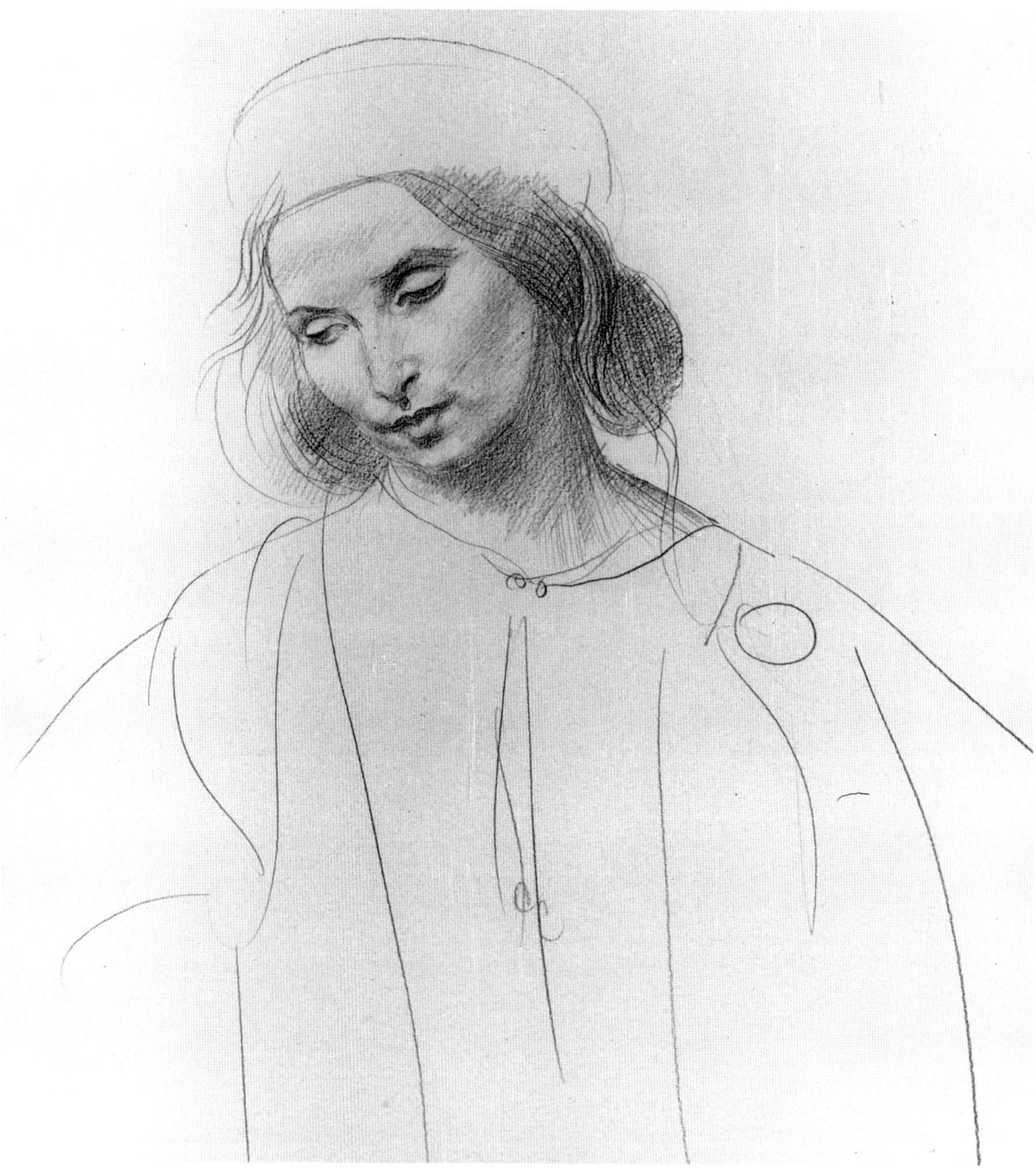

53

Between 1903 and 1914 Dorelia was central to John's work. With the advent of war and the commissioned portraits of the 1920s, she ceased to model for him, only to re-emerge exclusively in oil paintings in the late 1930s and thereafter occasionally in old age. This pair are among the finest drawings John ever made of Dorelia. They are exceptionally finely worked, and were clearly made in succession, the sitter removing her cap and cloak between poses. A third drawing (exh. London 1948, no.120) precedes Cat.53. The pose of Cat.54 anticipates the oil portrait of 1911 in the National Museum and Gallery, Cardiff (exh. Cardiff 1988, p.23 and no.19).

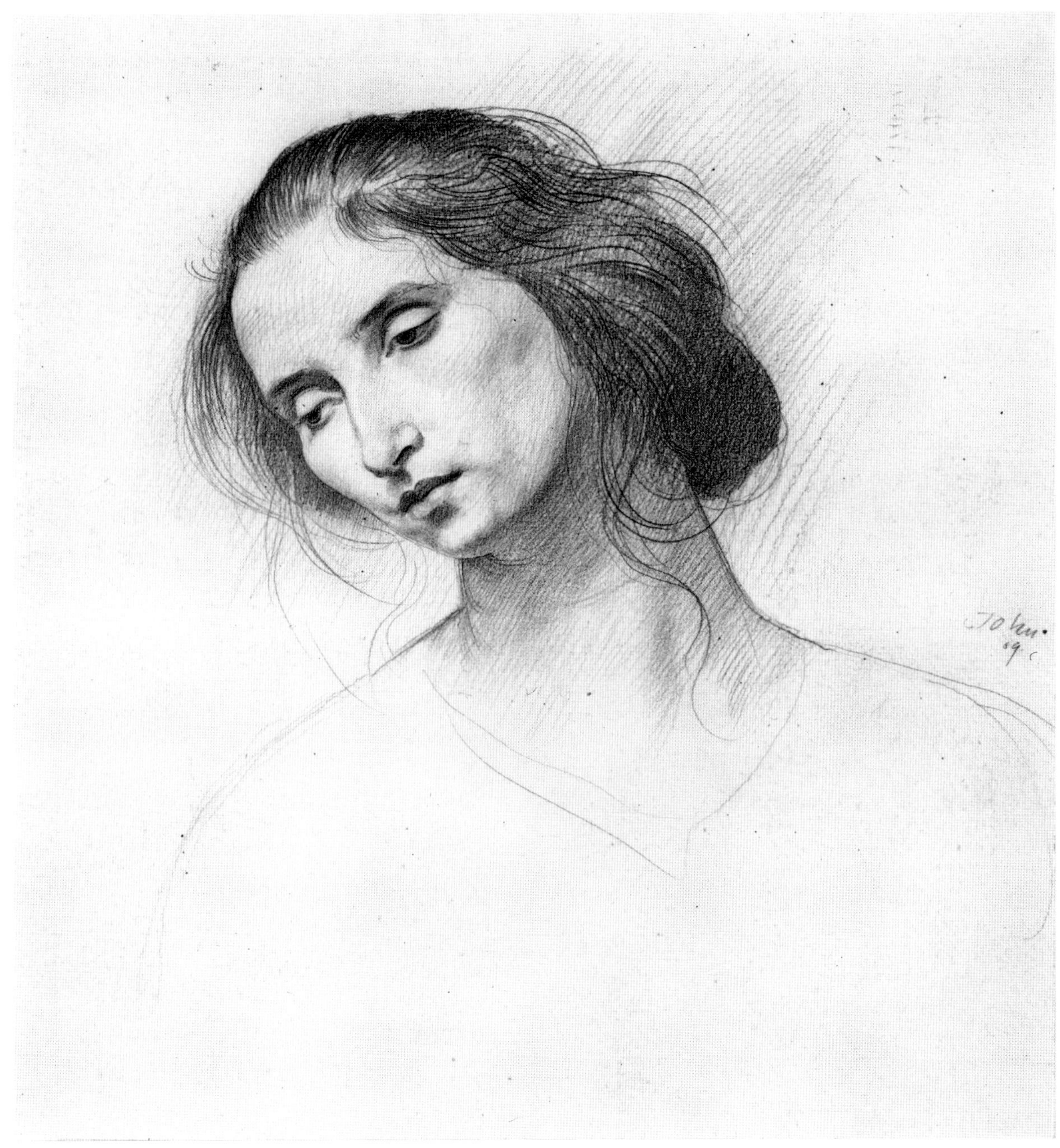

54

53 *Head of Dorelia wearing a cap*
pencil, 30.5×26.7 cm (12×10½ in)
LIT: exh. London 1954, no.91
PROV: Purchased from the artist
Collection of the late Morton H. Sands

54 *Head of Dorelia, 1909*
pencil, 26.3×16.5 cm (10⅜×6½ in)
Signed: *John 09* (centre right)
PROV: Vernon Wethered; J. L. W. Bird
Fine Art
Private Collection

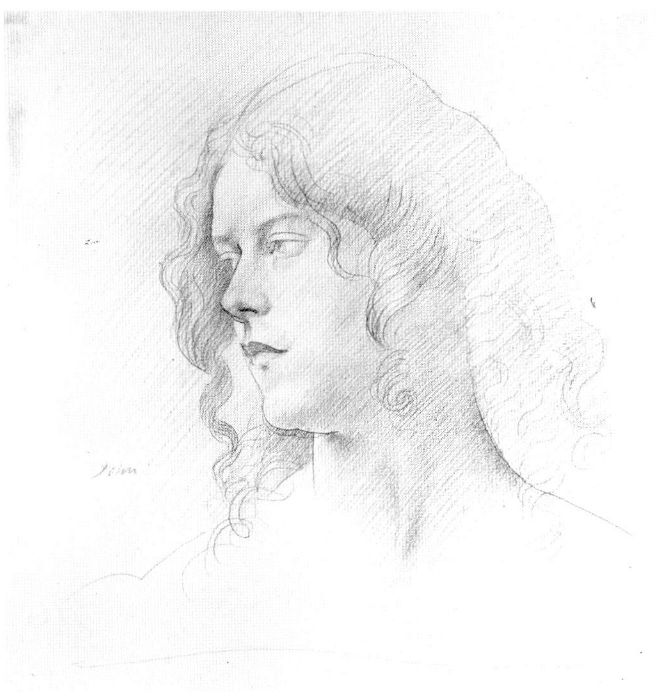

55

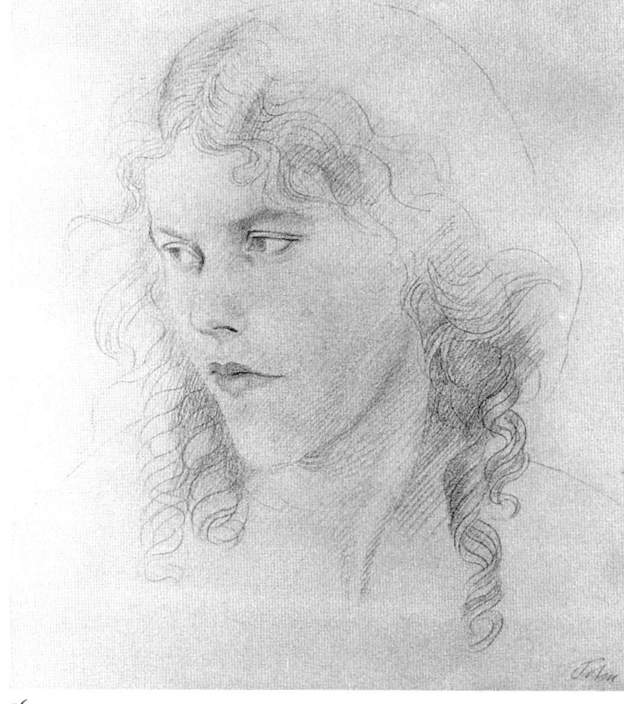

56

At least eleven portrait drawings of this
model were executed from varying
angles, using controlled diagonal
shading, running downwards from right
to left. The effect of this 'veiling', which
John employed repeatedly in drawings of
Alick Schepeler, is to soften the features
of a not especially elegant model, who
married the painter Derwent Lees (1885-
1931) in 1913 (Holroyd 1996, p.394). In
his vivid oil paintings she usually
appears as a big-boned country girl in
the landscape settings of Wales or
Southern France (see exh. Llandudno
1982, no.60).

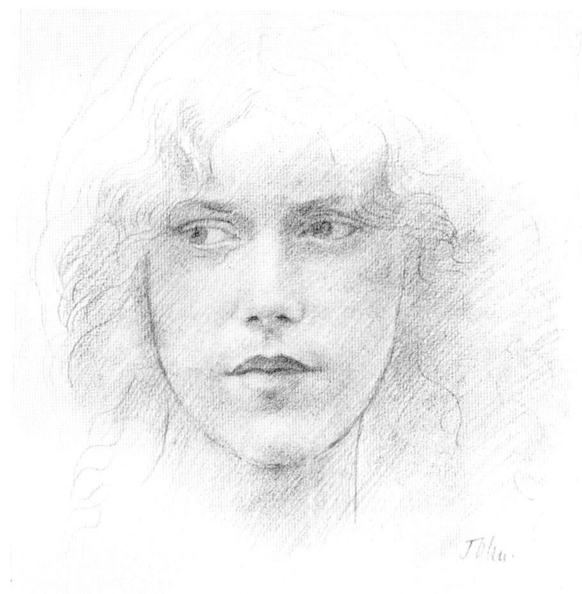

57

55 *Portrait of Mrs Derwent Lees*
pencil, 27.6×25.5 cm (10$\frac{7}{8}$×10 in)
Signed: *John* (lower left)
LIT: exh. London 1954, no.257;
Longstreet 1967, p.23; exh. Cambridge
1978, no.62
PROV: Dr Louis C. G. Clarke; by whom
bequeathed, 1961
Lent by the Syndics of the Fitzwilliam
Museum, Cambridge (PD.170-1961)

56 *Lyndra*
pencil, 32×28 cm (12$\frac{5}{8}$×11 in)
Signed: *John* (bottom right)
LIT: exh. London 1954, no.77;
*Contemporary Art Society for Wales 50th
Anniversary Exhibition*, National Museum
of Wales, Cardiff 1987, p.20 and no.21
PROV: Purchased by Lord Howard de
Walden for the Contemporary Art
Society for Wales, 1942/3 (no.21); by
whom placed on permanent loan, 1947
Lent by CASW and the Glynn Vivian Art
Gallery, Swansea (GV 1947-1019)

57 *Head of Edith Lees*
pencil, 22.9×21.6 cm (9×8$\frac{1}{2}$ in)
Signed: *John* (bottom right)
PROV: T. W. Bacon
Private Collection

58 *Study of a woman's head, 1910*
pencil, 40.6×25.4 cm (16×10 in)
Signed: *John/1910* (centre right)
LIT: exh. Cambridge 1978, no.61
PROV: Sir Herbert Thompson; by whom
presented, 1920
Lent by the Syndics of the Fitzwilliam
Museum, Cambridge (No.1025)

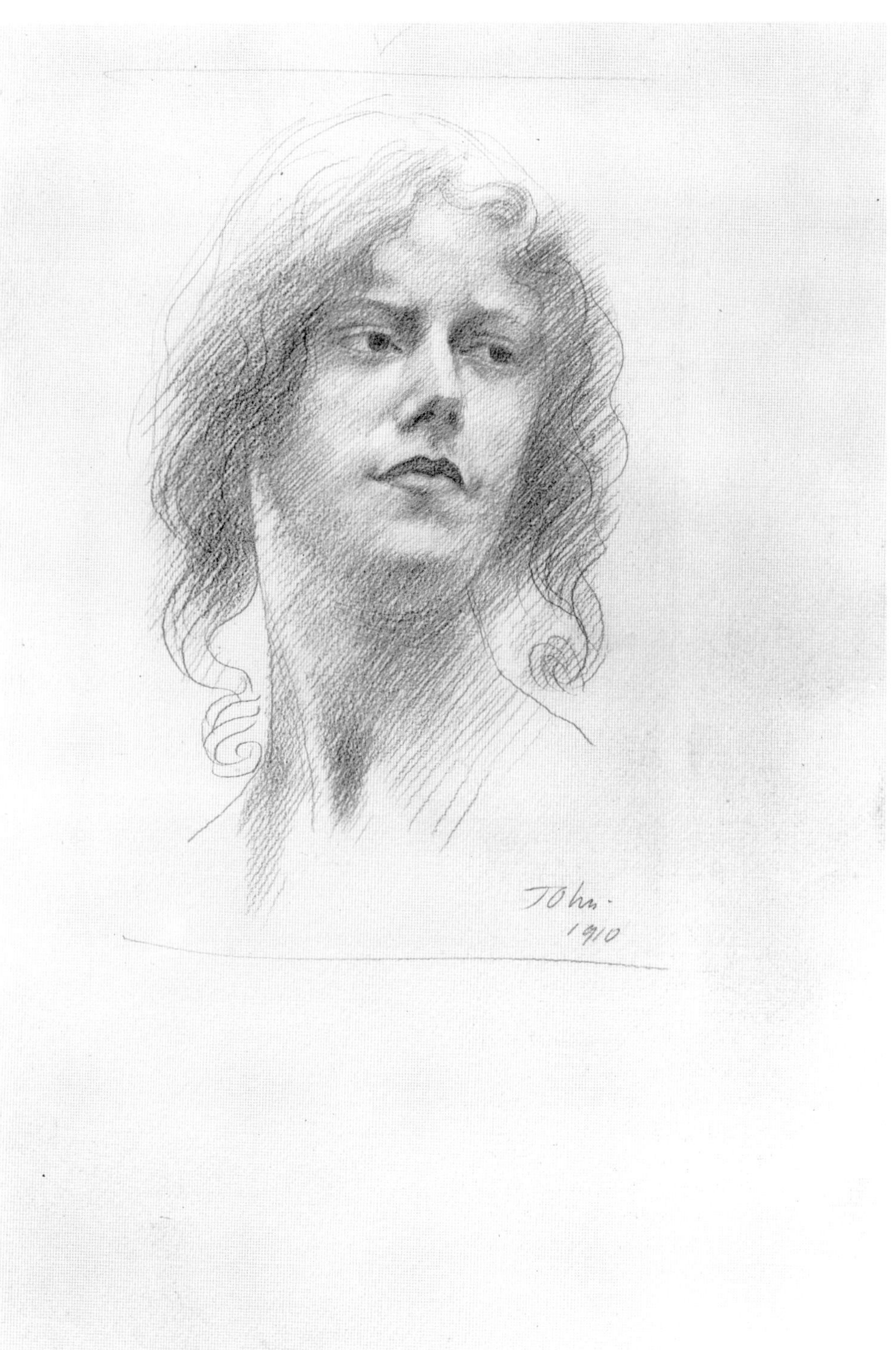

58

Robin John standing, *c.*1910

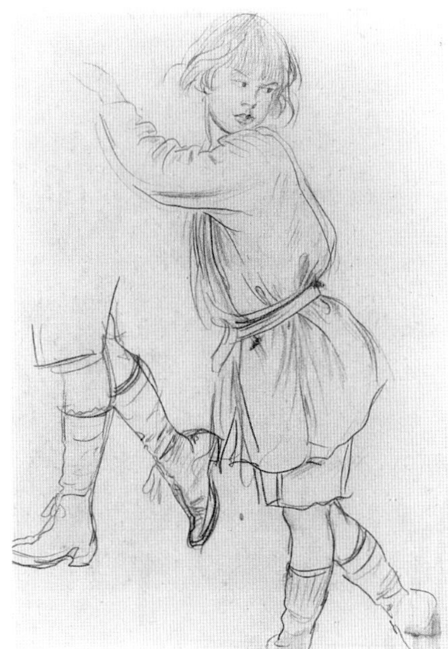

Fig.7 *Robin, studies*, pencil, whereabouts unknown

Robin John (1904-88) inspired some of his father's most beautiful child portraiture, but he had a fairly disastrous relationship with him and grew up a loner, living abroad – in Jamaica, Florida and Spain – returning to England very rarely. He had a varied career and became a linguist, but was famously silent in all seven languages he learned (Holroyd 1996, p.539). In this drawing and a closely-related work (Fig.7, whereabouts unknown), John has caught the twists and turns of a child at play. The home-made smock is worn just as Ida had advised Robin's elder brother David in 1907: 'You put the belt around, rather low down, and pull the coat out evenly all round' (Aberystwyth, National Library of Wales, NLW MS 22798B, f.8).

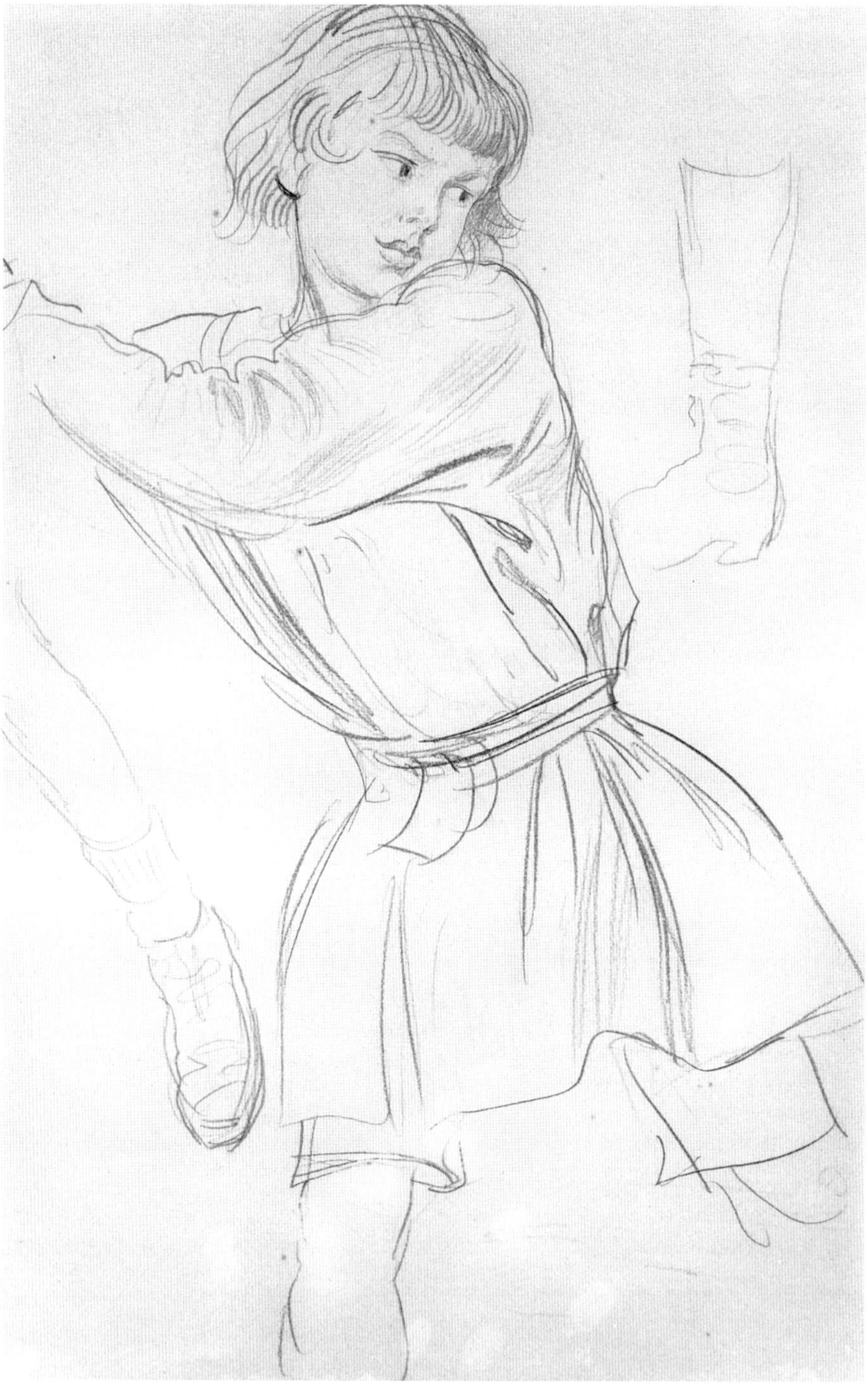

59

59 *The artist's son Robin, studies*
pencil, 38.7×24.2 cm (15$\frac{1}{4}$×9$\frac{1}{2}$ in)
Lent by NatWest Group Art Collection
(M440)

Galway: Shawled girls, 1915

Having been declared medically unfit for military service, John visited the west coast of Ireland in 1915. He described Galway: '… bevies of shawled, barefooted girls passed, laughing, as we threaded the labyrinthine streets which resounded with the cries of fish-women: somewhere a voice, sweetened by distance, wailed nostalgically: "Eileen allanah, Eileen asthore!" … women still lingered, murmuring by the Spanish Gate – a face, or part of a face, blooming for an instant from shadowy veils and quickly averted. The Claddagh in the half-light begins to look unsubstantial and dream-like …' (*Autobiography*, p.107). John utilised this group of figures in his oil *Cartoon for Galway* (Tate Gallery), first exhibited at the Royal Academy in 1916 (see Easton and Holroyd 1974, no.57). These expressionistic drawings of urban poor contrast with his idyllic watercolours of rural life in Galway (Cats 64-7).

60 *Galway peasants*
faded blue ink and wash, 45.6×31.5 cm (18×12½ in)
LIT: *Catalogue of the Gwendoline E. Davies Bequest*, National Museum of Wales, Cardiff 1952, no.48
PROV: Bequeathed by Gwendoline Davies, 1952
National Museum and Gallery, Cardiff (NMW A3664)

61 *Galway shawls*
ink and wash, 45.6 x. 31.6 cm (18×12½ in)
Signed: *John* (bottom right)
PROV: A. E. Anderson; by whom presented through the National Art-Collections Fund, 1923
Lent by the Whitworth Art Gallery, University of Manchester (D.1923.19)

62 *Donegal shawls*
faded blue ink and washes, 44.4×30.5 cm (17½×12 in)
Signed: *John* (bottom left)
LIT: exh. London 1948, no.93; *Catalogue of the Gwendoline E. Davies Bequest*,

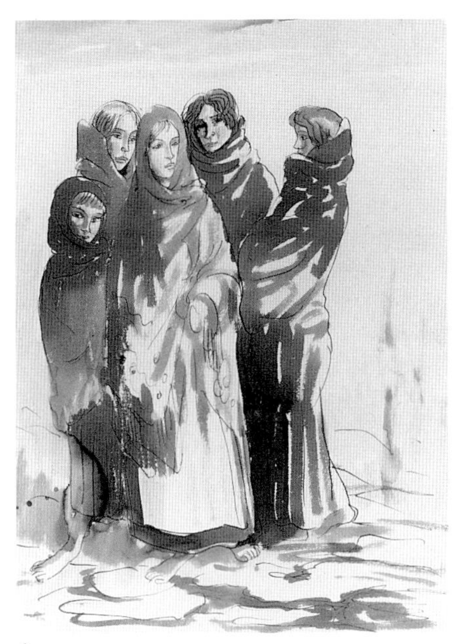

60

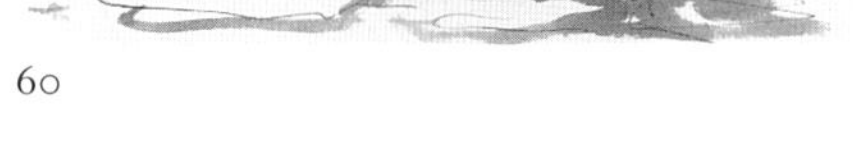

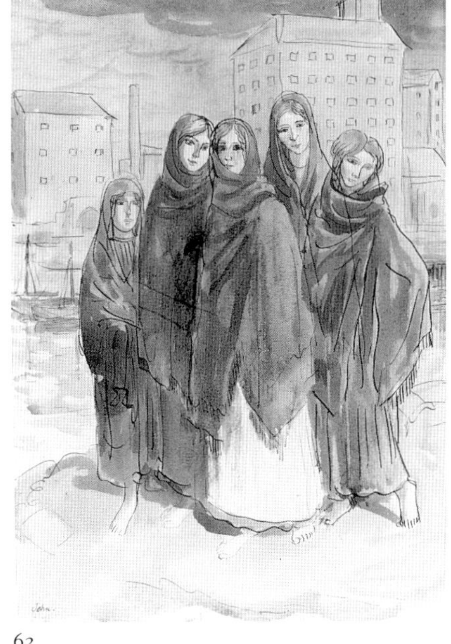

62

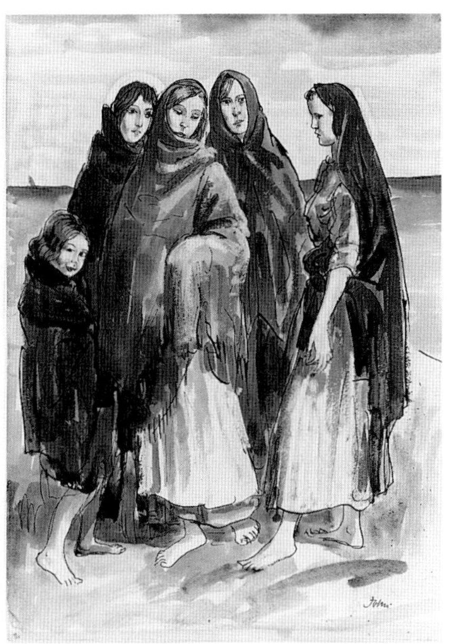

61

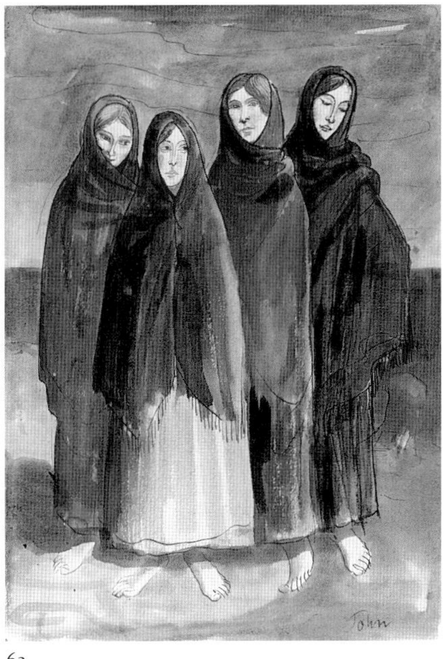

63

National Museum of Wales, Cardiff 1952, no.59
PROV: T. Sands Johnson; Hugh Blaker; Gwendoline Davies; by whom bequeathed, 1952
National Museum and Gallery, Cardiff (NMW A3663)

63 *Fish wives of the west*
ink and wash, 45.6×31.6 cm (18×12½ in)
Signed: *John* (bottom right)
PROV: Independent Gallery; from whom purchased, 1923
Lent by the Whitworth Art Gallery, University of Manchester (D.1923.34)

Galway: Peasants, 1915

John spent two months sketching the 'shawlies' and fisher families of Galway, although his presence was regarded with suspicion (was he a wartime spy?), and he spent a good deal of time dodging policemen and drawing from memory indoors (Holroyd 1996, p.406). He produced numerous pen and ink studies in this way, relieved, perhaps from the discipline of drawing endless beautifully poised women. He could indulge in a grumpy expression, an awkward body; a caricature, and have a joke. In Cat.64 the crossed-out head of a fifth figure indicates that it precedes Cat.65, where a black-shawled figure is introduced, and combined with the woman wearing a speckled jacket (Cat.66). An ink drawing of another group of figures (Fig.8, whereabouts unknown) precedes Cat.67, in which the bright, un-naturalistic colouring is consistent with the primitive handling of the figures. His 'Galway peasants' grouped against 'the speckled mountains of Connemara' which he had seen in the distance from the Aran Islands, may represent the islanders themselves. John later mused: 'Who were these people? Formorians, Milesians, Tuatha-de-Danaan, Firbolg?' (*Autobiography*, p.109). And who were *they*?

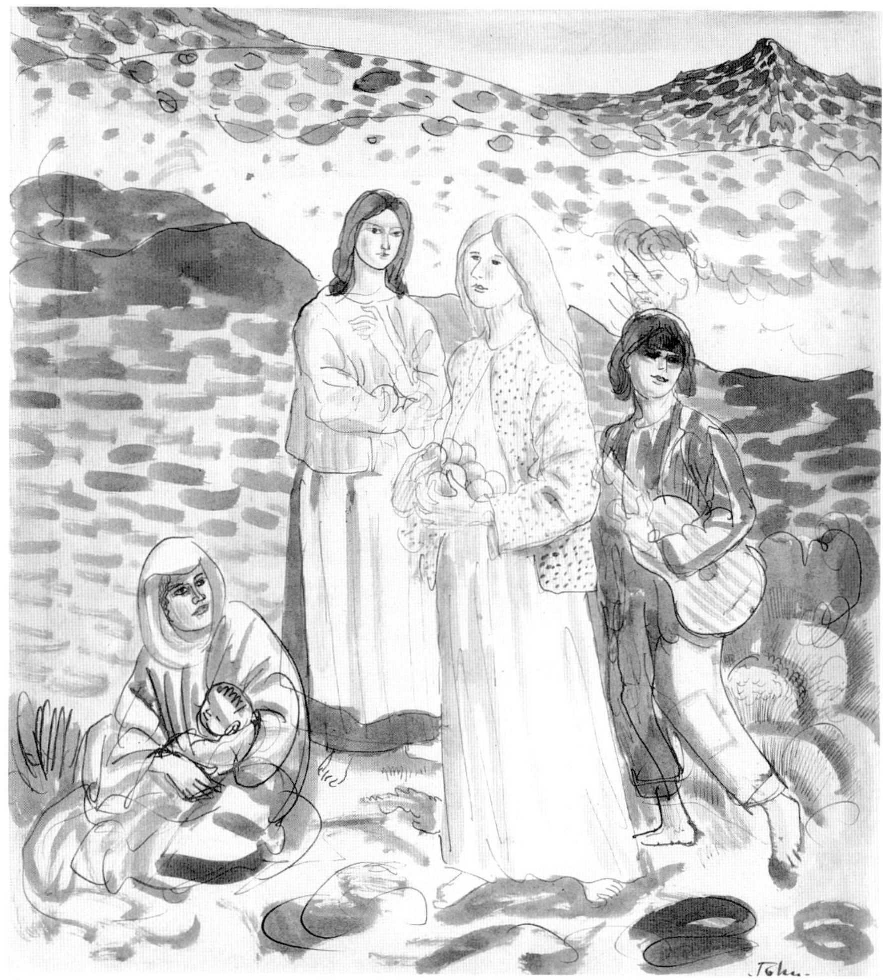

64

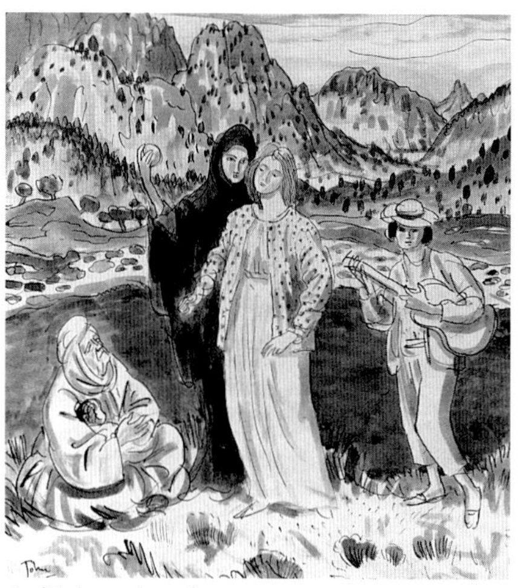

65 (Colour plate 6)

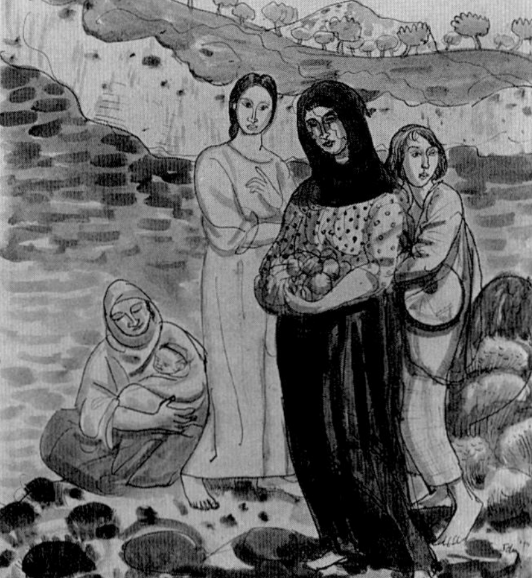

66

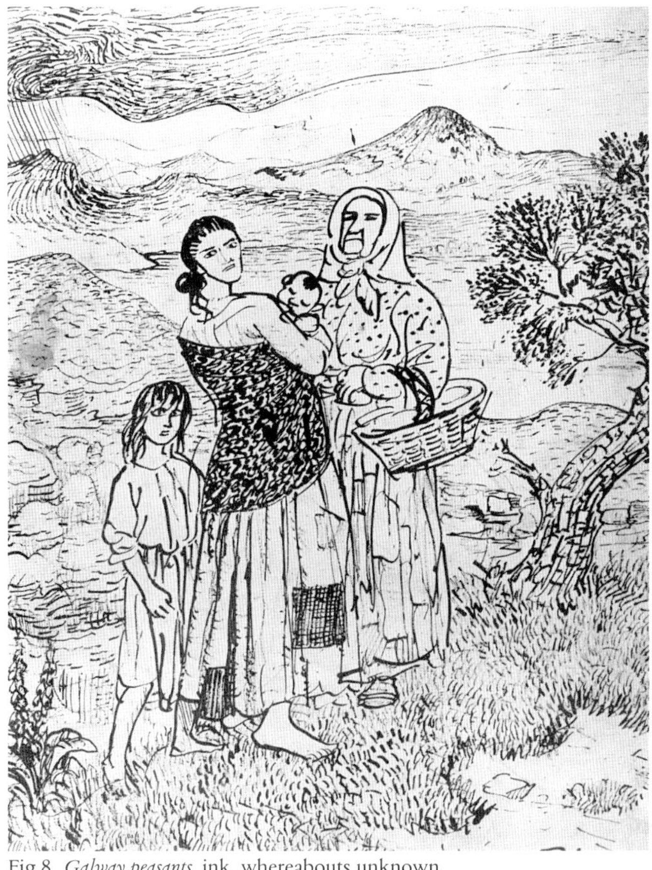

Fig.8 *Galway peasants*, ink, whereabouts unknown

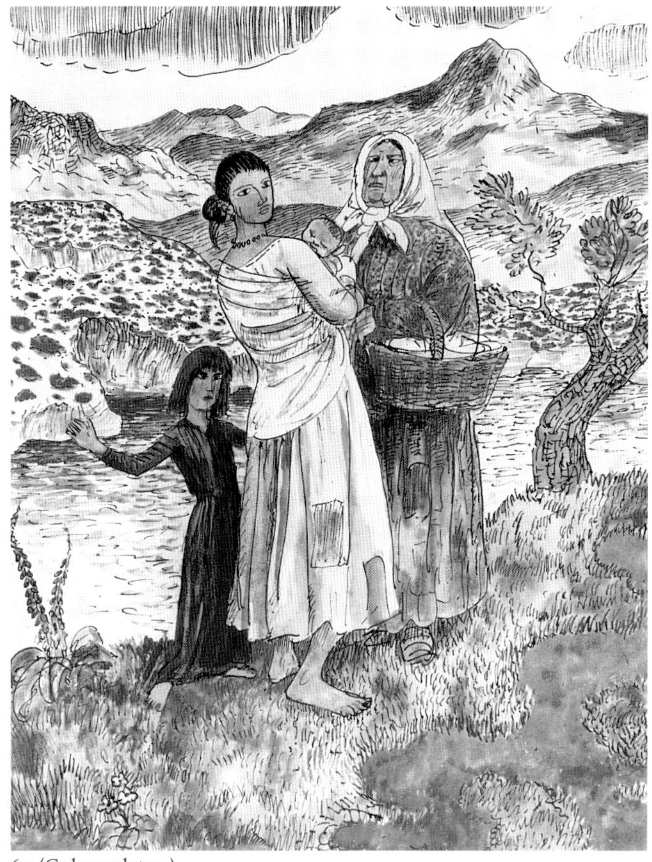

67 (Colour plate 7)

64 *Galway peasants*
indian ink and grey wash on discoloured
paper, 45.7×40.7 cm (18×16 in)
Signed: *John* (bottom right)
LIT: exh. London 1954, no.296;
Longstreet 1967, p.19; exh. Cambridge
1978, no.66
PROV: Christie's 6 February 1917; bought
by Sir Alec Martin; by whom given, 1917
Lent by the Syndics of the Fitzwilliam
Museum, Cambridge (No.854)

65 *Le Paradou*
ink and wash, 45.7×40.7 cm (18×15½ in)
Signed: *John / 1915* (bottom left)
LIT: Browse 1942, no.48; exh. London
1948, no.97; London 1954, no.300
PROV: Sir James Murray; from whom
purchased
Lent by City of Aberdeen Art Gallery
(ABDAG003086)

66 *The black shawl*
ink and wash, 45.8×40.5 cm (18×16 in)
Signed: *John / 1915* (bottom right)
PROV: A. E. Anderson; by whom
presented through the National Art-
Collections Fund, 1926
Lent by the Whitworth Art Gallery,
University of Manchester (D.1926.35)

67 *Galway peasants*
ink and watercolour, 50.8×38.1 cm
(20×15 in)
Signed: *John* (bottom centre right)
LIT: exh. London 1948, no.99 (mistitled
Peasants in the Pyrenees)
PROV: W. A. Evill
Private Collection

Madame Suggia, 1921-3

By the 1920s John had become as
famous as many of his sitters and was
deluged with a growing demand for
commissioned portraits. Some sat
nervously, others willingly. The
distinguished Portuguese cellist
Guilhermina Suggia (1888-1950) was
enthusiastic, and collaborated closely
with the artist throughout the two and a
half years her portrait took to complete.
The initial challenge was to establish her
pose (the finer details of the bow-hold
and the painting of the Montagnana
cello presented no less of a challenge),
and the solution was to catch her head in
profile with eyes closed, thereby
avoiding the problem of facial
movements made by musicians while
playing. The surviving studies
concentrate on the turn of her head. In
the final painting (Tate Gallery) John
decided on a turn to the right, which
freed the sitter's profile from the cello's
head (Fig.9, Tate Gallery).

68 *Guilhermina Suggia, three-quarters to left*
black chalk, 45.7×30.5 cm (18×12 in)
LIT: exh. Cardiff 1988, no.34
PROV: Dorelia John; from whose estate
purchased, 1972
National Museum and Gallery, Cardiff
(NMW A1846)

69 *Guilhermina Suggia, profile to right*
black chalk, 34.9×29.8 cm ($13\frac{3}{4}$×$11\frac{3}{4}$ in)
Inscribed: *Mde Suggia* (lower right)
Signed: *John* (bottom right)
PROV: Mrs Thelma Cazalet-Keir CBE
Private Collection

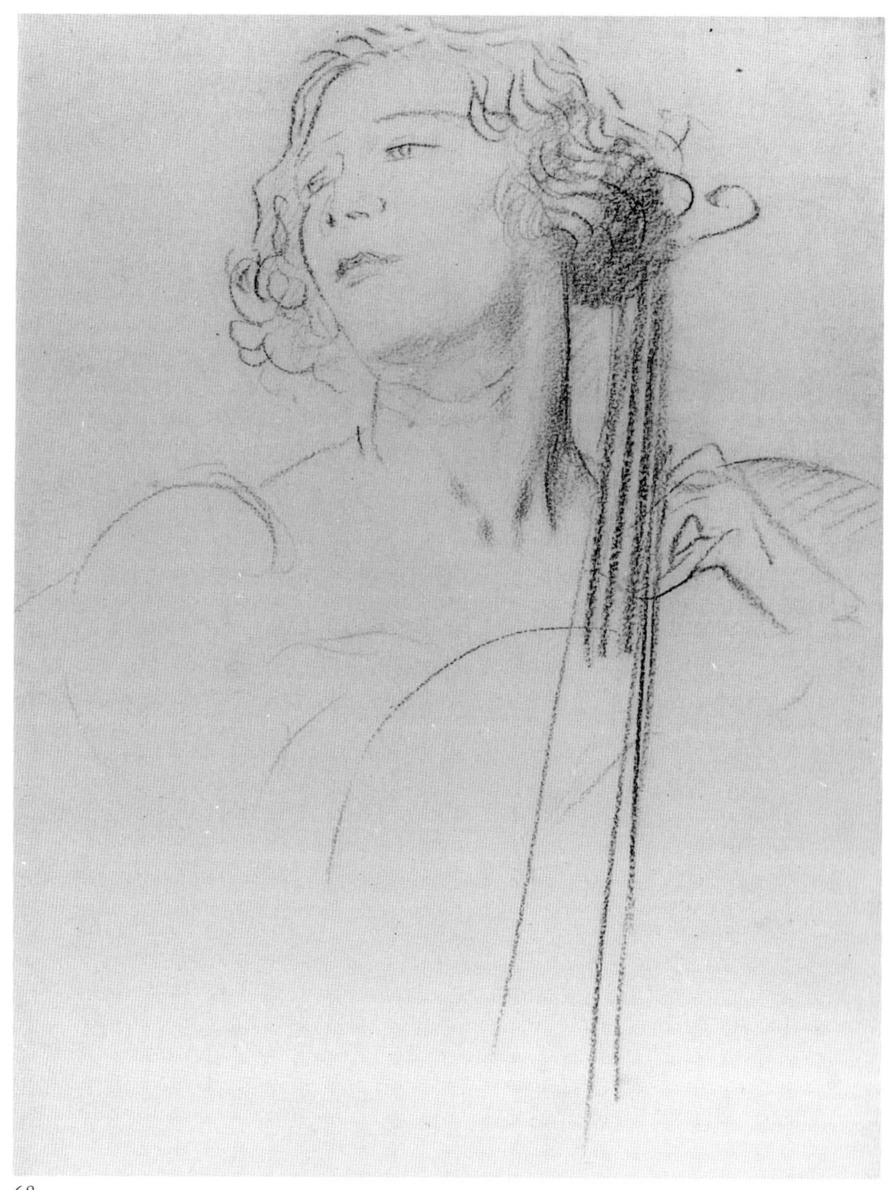

68

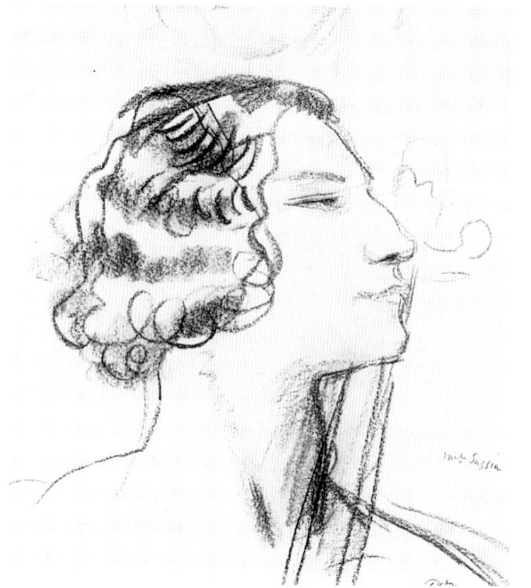

69

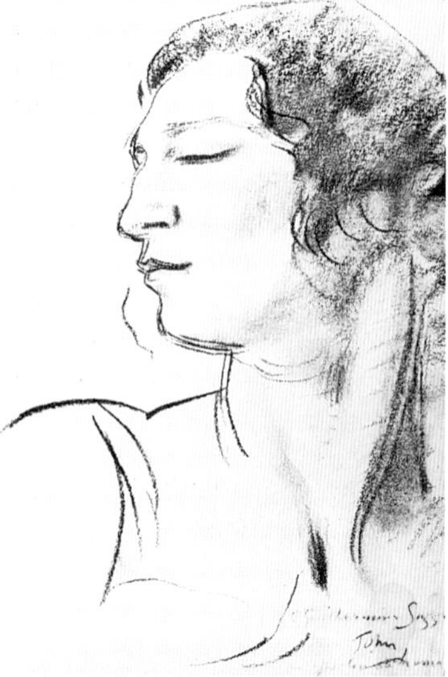

Fig.9 *Guilhermina Suggia*, charcoal,
Tate Gallery

Romilly John, 1931

This series of heads of the artist's son
aged twenty-five was made for Romilly's
book of *Poems* published in 1931. A sixth
version (private collection) was used for
the frontispiece. The following year saw
the publication of *The Seventh Child*, a
sensitive account of his childhood and
young manhood. Romilly (1906-86) was
the gentlest natured of John's sons and
looked after Dorelia in her old age.
These portraits reflect his meditative
mood. They signify a return to the
mixed use of black and red chalk, which
the artist had abandoned around 1910,
and anticipate the looser, woollier style
of the late portrait drawings of the 1930s
and 1940s. Other drawings of this
period have a more sculptural quality,
signalling his experiments with clay
sculpture during the 1950s, his last
working decade.

70 *Romilly John*
black chalk, 26×19.7 cm (10¼×7¾ in)
Inscribed: *Romilly* (bottom right)
Signed: *John* (bottom right)
PROV: Mrs J. E. Fitzackerly; sold Christie's
2 March 1979, lot 46
Lent by Mr and Mrs Stephen Evans

71 *Romilly John*
black chalk, 26×19.7 cm (10¼×7¾ in)
Inscribed: *Romilly* (bottom right)
Signed: *John* (bottom right)
PROV: Mrs Thelma Cazalet-Keir CBE
Private Collection

72 *Romilly John*
red and black chalks, 28.5×22.8 cm
(11¼×9 in)
Signed: *John* (top right)
PROV: Christie's 9 June 1989, lot 272
Lent by Mrs Fiona Wright

73 *Romilly John, with hand on chin*
red and black chalks, 28×22.2 cm
(11×8¾ in)
Signed: *John* (bottom right)
PROV: Anthony D'Offay Gallery
Private Collection

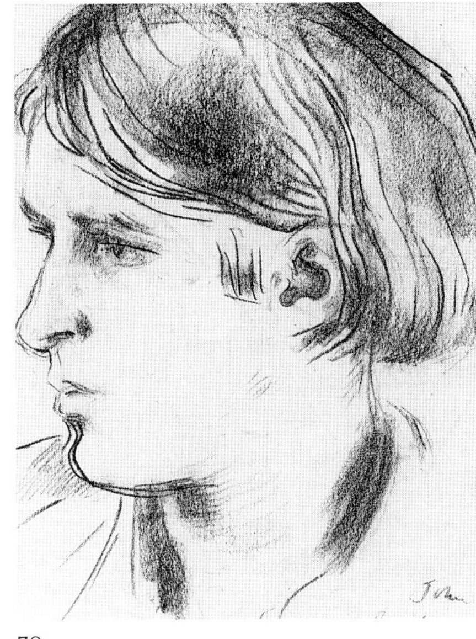

70

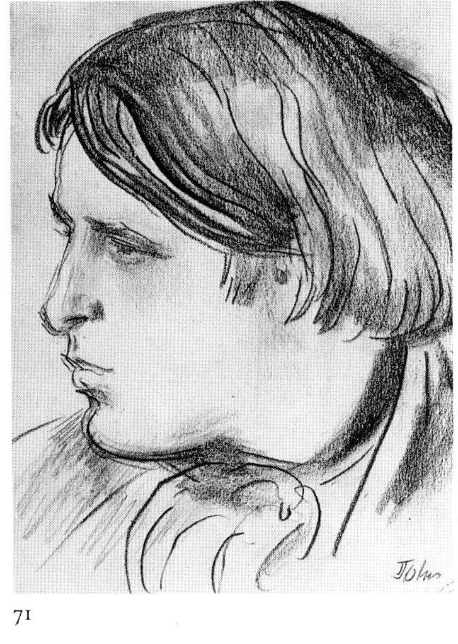

71

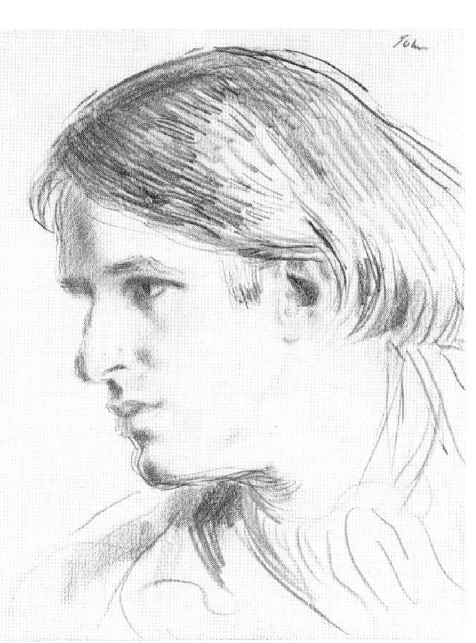

72

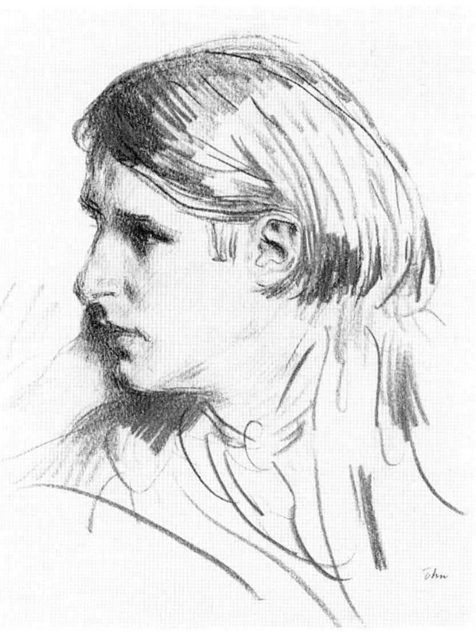

73

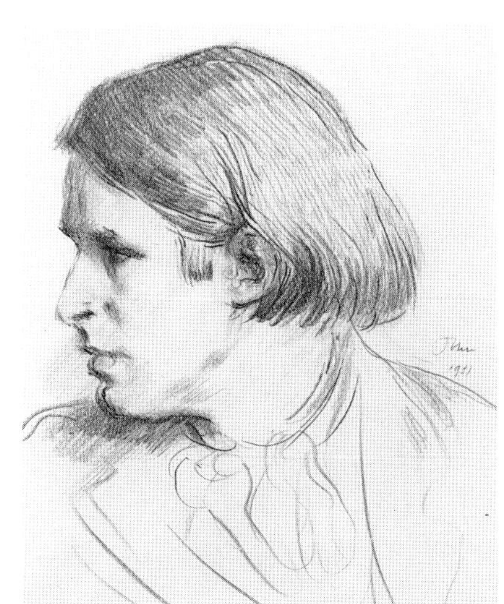

74 (Colour plate 8)

74 *Romilly John*
red and black chalks, 28×22.8 cm
(11×9 in)
Signed: *John / 1931* (centre right)
PROV: Executor of the late Romilly John,
sold Woolley & Wallis, Salisbury 15 April
1987, lot 257
Spink & Son Ltd

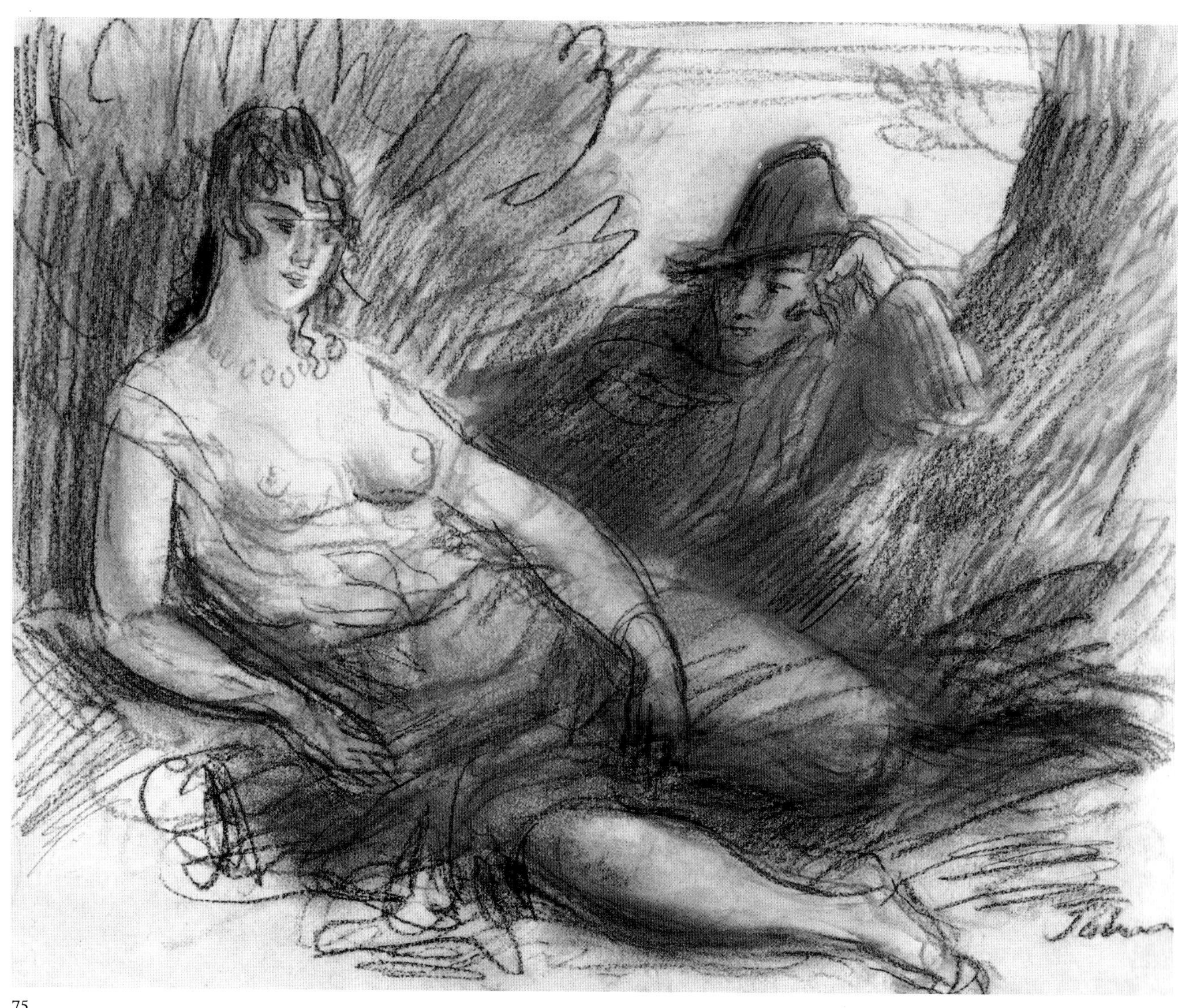

75

75 *Gypsy courtship*
red and black chalk, 22.9 × 27.9 cm
(9 × 11 in)
Signed: *John* (bottom right)
Lent by Dorothy Meade

76 *Atque in Arcadia Ego*
red and black chalk, 21.6 × 26 cm
($8\frac{1}{2} × 10\frac{1}{4}$ in)
Signed: *John* (bottom left)
LIT: Rothenstein 1944, no.71
PROV: Sotheby's 10 March 1982, lot 73;
Andrew Kimpton
Lent by John Mortimer

77 *Gypsy courtship*
black chalk on brownish discoloured
paper, 21.6 × 26.7 cm ($8\frac{1}{2} × 10\frac{1}{2}$ in)
Signed: *John* (bottom right)
Lent by Ben John

In the introduction to his book of
Romani Poems, published 'with English
Renderings' in 1931, John Sampson
wrote: 'Most of these poems were
written during the years when I was
collecting material for my monograph
on the speech of the Welsh Kalé, and
when, in Gypsy haunts and in Gypsy
company, Romani was constantly in my
thoughts and on my lips'. In an
unpublished memoir of his grandfather
Anthony Sampson describes the
commission for its frontispiece:

'… the Oxford University Press agreed
to publish his poems in Romani which
he had written twenty years before. He
again asked John for a frontispiece, who
agreed with his usual generosity; "Of
course I'd be sad to miss being in this
book, for our friendship has meant a
very great deal to me and our gypsying
together one of the major episodes in my
blooming life". He duly sent six
drawings of a Gypsy courtship which
"become more and more indecorous".
And he added: "I think perhaps the big
girl with a chap gazing at her and not
mauling her about would do best." The
Rai chose that one (now owned by my
sister) – a bosomy half-naked Gypsy girl
being watched by a gypsy boy – which
duly appeared opposite the title page of
the little book called: "Romane Gilia,
John Sampsoneste".'

These drawings demonstrate how John's
versions of the theme became 'more and
more indecorous', and Cat.75 is that used
in the frontispiece. Like those executed
thirty years earlier for *Omar Khayyam*
(Cats 1 and 2), they were done from the
imagination, and the theme of 'gypsy
courtship' strikes the same light-hearted
note of a couple enjoying themselves out
of doors.

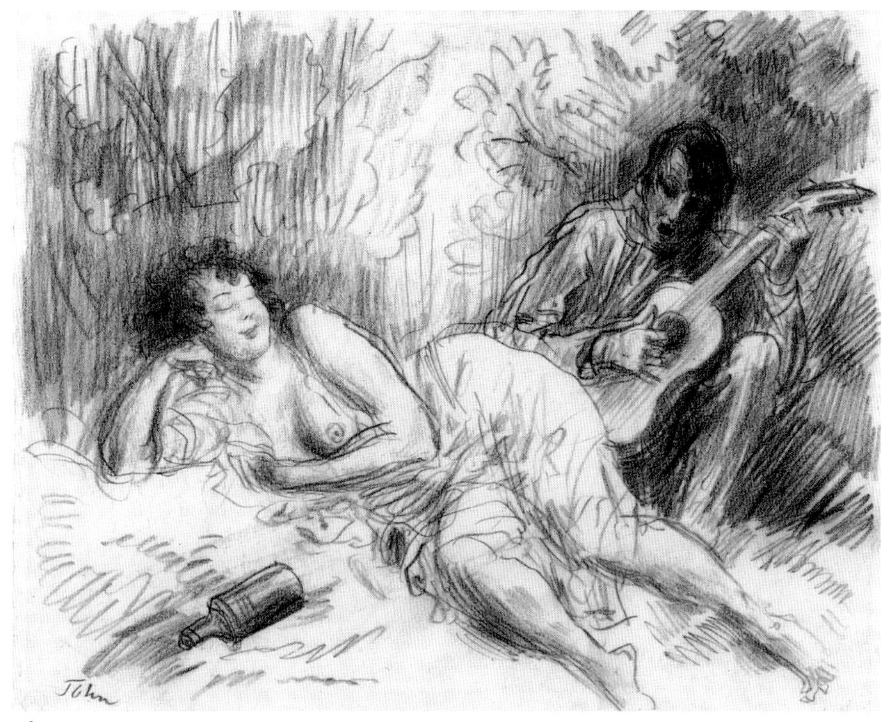

76

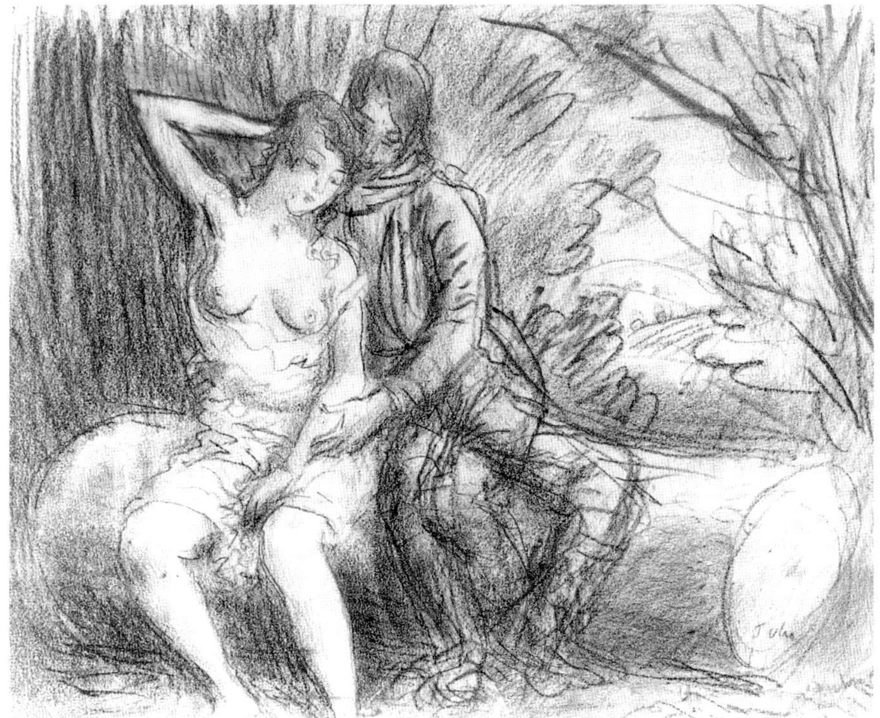

77

Augustus John, west of Ireland, 1930

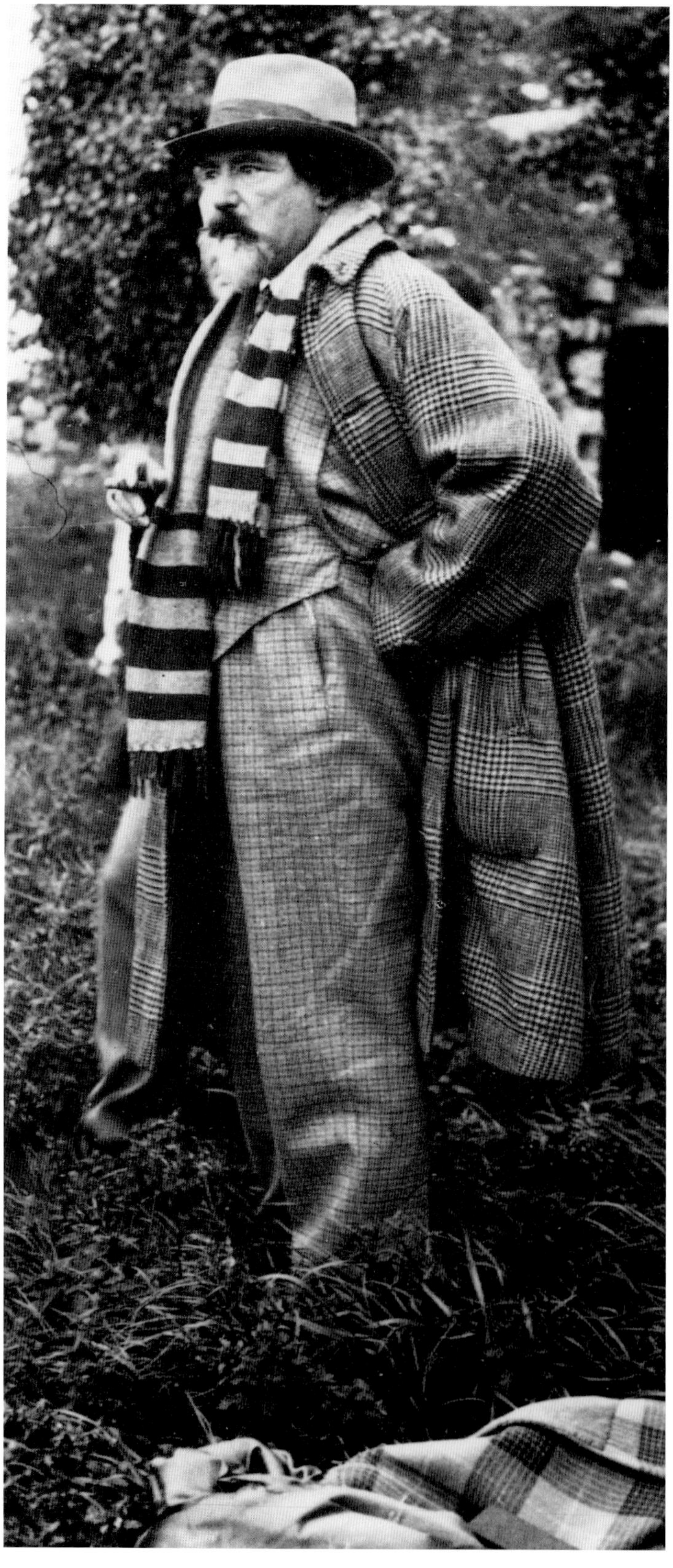

Select Bibliography

Books and articles

Harry Graf Kessler, 'Ein neuer englischer Künstler: A. E. John', *Kunst und Künstler*, 2, 1904, pp.360-3

Frank Rutter, 'Un artiste anglais: Augustus John', *L'Art et les Artistes*, 15, 1912, pp.161-8

Hugh Blaker, 'The Drawings of Augustus John', *Colour*, May 1916, p.122ff

Charles Marriott, *Augustus John*, London 1918

Campbell Dodgson, *A catalogue of etchings by Augustus John, 1901-14*, London 1920

Anthony Bertram, *Augustus John*, London 1923

Ettore Cosmati, 'Augustus John', *Dedalo*, 9, 1928-9, pp.677-705

Frank Rutter, 'Augustus John', *Studio*, 101, 1931, pp.84-97

Campbell Dodgson, 'Additions to the catalogue of etchings by Augustus John', *Print Collectors Quarterly*, 18, 1931, pp.270-87

T. W. Earp, *Augustus John*, Edinburgh and London 1934

Lillian Browse (ed.), *Augustus John: Drawings*, London 1941 (1st ed.), 1942 (2nd ed.)

John Rothenstein, *Augustus John*, London and New York 1944

John Rothenstein, *Modern English Painters*, vol.1, London 1952, pp.175-87

Denys Sutton, 'The significance of Augustus John', *Country Life*, 25 March 1954, p.866

Lord David Cecil (ed.), *Augustus John: Fifty-two drawings*, London 1957

Stephen Longstreet, *The Drawings of Augustus John*, Alhambra, Calif. 1967

Malcolm Easton, 'Augustus John: An artist and his family', *Connoisseur*, 175, October 1970, pp.88-93

Malcolm Easton, 'Dorelia's wardrobe', *Vogue*, August 1974, pp.78-9

Malcolm Easton and Michael Holroyd, *The Art of Augustus John*, London 1974

Michael Holroyd, *Augustus John*, vol.1, *The Years of Innocence*, London 1974 and vol.2, *The Years of Experience*, London 1975

Richard Shone, *Augustus John*, Oxford 1979

Michael Holroyd, *Augustus John. The New Biography*, London 1996

Exhibition and sale catalogues

London, Independent Gallery 1923. *Private collection of the earlier work of Augustus E. John*

London, Independent Gallery 1923. *Mr John Quinn's collection of the earlier drawings by Augustus John*

London, Redfern Gallery 1939. *Augustus John, J. D. Innes, Derwent Lees, Paintings 1910-14*

London, National Gallery 1940. *Drawings of Augustus John*

Leeds, Temple Newsam House 1946. *Paintings and drawings by Augustus John*

London, Arts Council of Great Britain 1948. *Drawings and Paintings by Augustus John*

New York, Scott and Fowles 1949. *Augustus John in American Collections*

London, Royal Academy 1954. *Works by Augustus John*

Sheffield, Graves Art Gallery 1956. *Augustus John*

London, Arthur Tooth and Sons Ltd 1961. *Paintings and drawings by Augustus John*

London, Christie's, 20 July 1962. *Drawings and Paintings from the Studio of the late Augustus John*, part I

London, Christie's, 21 June 1963, *Drawings and Paintings from the Studio of the late Augustus John*, part II

London, Upper Grosvenor Galleries 1965. *Drawings and murals by Augustus John*

London, Mercury Gallery 1968. *Augustus John Drawings*

Hull, University of Hull 1970. *Augustus John: portraits of the artist's family*

Halifax, Nova Scotia, Dalhousie Art Gallery 1972. *Augustus John*

London, Colnaghi & Co Ltd 1974. *Augustus John. Early drawings and etchings*

London, National Portrait Gallery 1975. *Augustus John*

Cardiff, National Museum of Wales 1978. *Augustus John: Studies for Compositions*

Cambridge, Fitzwilliam Museum 1978. *Augustus Edwin John, OM (1879-1961)*

Llandudno, Mostyn Art Gallery 1982. *Some Miraculous Promised Land. J. D. Innes, Augustus John and Derwent Lees in North Wales, 1910-13*

Cardiff, National Museum of Wales 1988. *Portraits by Augustus John: Family, Friends and the Famous*

London, Piccadilly Gallery in association with Max Rutherston 1991. *Augustus John: A collection of oils, drawings and etchings*

Publications by Augustus John and memoirs

Augustus John, 'The Paintings of Evan Walters', 'The
Unknown Artist', 'The Woman Artist', 'Paris and the
Painter', 'Three English Artists', 'Some Contemporary
French Painters', 'Five Modern Artists', 'Interior Decoration',
Vogue, 11 January 1928, p.40ff, 7 March 1928, p.53ff, 18 April
1928, p.50ff, 27 June 1928, p.46ff, 25 July 1928, p.44ff, 22
August 1928, p.36ff, 3 October 1928, p.76ff, 31 October
1928, p.51ff

Sir William Rothenstein, *Men and Memories*, vol.1, London 1931
and vol.2, London 1932

Romilly John, *The Seventh Child*, London 1932, reprinted with
additions, 1975

Augustus John, 'A Note on Holbein', *The Burlington Magazine*,
vol.78, January 1941, pp.265-6

Augustus John, 'A Note on Rembrandt', *The Burlington
Magazine*, vol.81, December 1942, p.290

Augustus John, *Chiaroscuro*, London 1952 (Published with
alterations from articles in *Horizon*, 1941-6)

R. Gathorne-Hardy (ed.), *Ottoline, The Early Memoirs of Lady
Ottoline Morrell*, London 1963

Augustus John, *Finishing Touches*, London 1964

Sir John Rothenstein, *Brave day, hideous night*, London 1966

Nicolette Devas, *Two Flamboyant Fathers*, London 1966

Augustus John, *Autobiography*, London 1975